Leckie ✕ Leckie

HIGHER

Modern Studies

grade **booster**

Guch Dhillon ✕ Joanne Kerr ✕ Wilma Simpson

Text © Wilma Simpson, Guch Dhillon and Joanne Kerr
Design and layout © 2008 Leckie & Leckie
Cover image © Caleb Rutherford

02/241108

ISBN 978-1-84372-378-3

Published by
Leckie & Leckie Ltd, 3rd floor, 4 Queen Street, Edinburgh, EH2 1JE
Tel: 0131 220 6831 Fax: 0131 225 9987
enquiries@leckieandleckie.co.uk   www.leckieandleckie.co.uk

Special thanks to
Pumpkin House (illustration), BRW (design and page makeup),
Roda Morrison (copy-editing), Caleb Rutherford (cover-design), Jill Laidlaw (proofreading),
Alan Barclay (content review).

A CIP Catalogue record for this book is available from the British Library.

® Leckie & Leckie is a registered trademark
Leckie & Leckie Ltd is a division of Huveaux plc.

Leckie & Leckie makes every effort to ensure that all paper used in our books is made from wood pulp obtained from well-managed forests, controlled sources and recycled wood or fibre.

Acknowledgements
Leckie & Leckie has made every effort to trace all copyright holders.
If any have been inadvertently overlooked, we will be pleased to make the necessary arrangements.

We would like to thank the following for permission to reproduce their material:
SQA for permission to reproduce past examination questions
(answers do not emanate from the SQA).
The article: 'The biggest poll debacle in the history of British democracy sees up to one in ten votes thrown out' (p. 17) is reproduced with the permission of The Scotsman.
The article: 'High number of spoiled papers puts spotlight on new system' (p. 17) is reproduced with the permission of The Herald, Glasgow © 2008 Herald & Times Group.

CONTENTS

1 Introduction

WHAT WILL I LEARN FROM THIS BOOK?

You will learn about the skills you need to achieve the best possible grade in Higher Modern Studies. You will learn how to answer the types of questions you will be asked in the examination and unit assessments. You will also learn how to answer evaluating questions and produce a report for a Decision Making Exercise. There are worked examples of answers, as well as hints and tips that will show you how to boost your grade.

HOW WILL THIS BOOK HELP ME?

This book will take you stage by stage through the skills you need for your Modern Studies course and both papers of the examination. It will also help you prepare for your National Assessment Bank (NAB) unit assessments. It will give you advice and answer many of the questions you have about how to do well in Higher Modern Studies.

THE COURSEWORK AND THE EXAMINATION

The Higher Modern Studies coursework comprises three units, all of which involve internal assessments, called unit assessments (often referred to as 'NABs'). The following table sets out the unit assessment requirements for Higher Modern Studies:

Unit assessments

Unit Number	Title	Internal Assessment
Unit 1	Political Issues in the United Kingdom	**Essay** on one of the study themes 35 minutes – pass/fail
Unit 2	Social Issues in the United Kingdom	**Decision Making Report** 1 hour – pass/fail
Unit 3	International Issues	**Essay** on one of the study themes 35 minutes – pass/fail

The examination

Exam Title	Task	Time
Paper 1	Four essays worth 15 marks each One from units 1, 2 and 3 and one more from unit 1 or 3	90 minutes
Paper 2	Decision Making Exercise based on unit 2 Two written sources, three statistical sources Evaluating questions worth total of 10 marks Decision Making Report worth 20 marks	75 minutes

WHAT'S IN THIS BOOK?

This introduction gives you general information about your examination.

Chapter 1 focuses on the skills you need. The chapter is divided into sections covering each of the skills. There are practical examples of techniques you can use to develop your Modern Studies skills.

Chapter 2 focuses on Paper 1, for which you have to write four analytical essays. The chapter is divided into sections covering:

> *The examination paper*
> *Timing*
> *The essay structure*
> *The essay questions*
> *Writing an essay*
> *Marking essays*
> *Essay marking grid*

The examples are from the most popular study themes.

Chapter 3 focuses on Paper 2, for which you have to use written and statistical sources to answer evaluating questions and write a Decision Making Report. The chapter is divided into sections covering:

> *The examination paper*
> *Timing*
> *The evaluating questions*
> *The Decision Making Task*
> *Planning the report*
> *Writing the report*
> *Marking the report*
> *Report marking grid*

There are highlighted sections giving you handy hints and tips for preparing for, and sitting, your examination and each chapter has a glossary of terms used.

HOW SHOULD I USE THIS BOOK?

This book can help you at various points in your course. Dip into it when you need to. But make sure you come back and study it more thoroughly when you prepare for your exam. That's when you will find the advice, tips and skills in the book really useful!

1 Modern Studies Skills

Introduction

Reading for information

Note taking

Keeping up-to-date

Analysing and evaluating

Data handling

Effective writing

Glossary

INTRODUCTION

This chapter shows you how to develop the skills you need for Higher Modern Studies.

In Higher Modern Studies you are assessed on knowledge and understanding, analysis and evaluating. You can develop skills to boost your grade in each of these. For example:

	Skill	Helps you to
Knowledge and understanding	Reading for information Note taking	Give accurate and extended descriptions and refer to complex factors
Analysis	Keeping up-to-date Showing balance Reaching conclusions	Give detailed explanations and refer to different points of view
Evaluating	Detecting bias Synthesis Data handling	Give detailed examples and well-developed conclusions
	Effective writing	Put information together in well-written, well-argued essays and reports

READING FOR INFORMATION

Reading will form an important part of the Modern Studies Course at Higher. Candidates should be encouraged to read and spend time on skills such as speed reading.

Higher Modern Studies Conditions and Arrangements

By developing this skill you will gather good information to boost your grade in knowledge and understanding. The best way to read for information is to read actively.

If you read actively you retain information for longer. There are three stages to reading actively – **Preview, Read** and **Recall**.

You preview to see what the text is about and how it is organised. This helps you decide how difficult it is and how long it will take to read.

How do I preview?

Quickly look at ...

● Title	... to get an idea of what the text is about
● Introduction	... to get the main ideas
● Sub-headings	... to see how these ideas are organised
● First sentences of paragraphs	... to see what that section is about
● Diagrams, maps, charts	... to see what examples are important
● Conclusions or summaries	... to see the relationship between the main ideas

At the same time, check for **reading aids** – italics, bold text, bullet points, number lists, side panels and questions at the end. These tell you the important points.

How do I read actively?

Read with a purpose and for each section ...

● Ask yourself a question and find the answer in the text.

● Underline or highlight key words and phrases.

● Jot down the main points or make notes in the margin (if you have permission to do this).

● Use a dictionary to look up any words you do not understand. If you think they will be useful, add them to your Modern Studies vocabulary list and use them in your answers.

How do I recall?

Transform the information by ...

- using your own words to answer questions about what you have just read
- making notes in your own words

How do I put this into practice?

The following example from *Higher Modern Studies Course Notes* by Leckie & Leckie shows you how to read for information.

EXAMPLE OF READING FOR INFORMATION

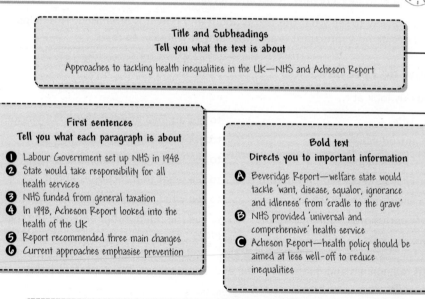

Title and Subheadings
Tell you what the text is about

Approaches to tackling health inequalities in the UK—NHS and Acheson Report

First sentences
Tell you what each paragraph is about

1. Labour Government set up NHS in 1948
2. State would take responsibility for all health services
3. NHS funded from general taxation
4. In 1998, Acheson Report looked into the health of the UK
5. Report recommended three main changes
6. Current approaches emphasise prevention

Bold text
Directs you to important information

A. Beveridge Report—welfare state would tackle 'want, disease, squalor, ignorance and idleness' from 'cradle to the grave'
B. NHS provided 'universal and comprehensive' health service
C. Acheson Report—health policy should be aimed at less well-off to reduce inequalities

Bulleted points
Summarise the main information

Acheson Report recommended:
- Increased benefits for mothers, children and elderly
- More money, better nutrition and health promotion for schools in poorer areas
- Ban on smoking and tobacco advertising, increasing price of tobacco and free nicotine replacement therapy on NHS

Side panel
Gives additional information about founding of NHS

Study Theme 2: Wealth and health inequalities in the UK

STRATEGIES TO DEAL WITH HEALTH INEQUALITIES

The NHS was introduced in 1948 by the Labour Government as a collectivist answer to health provision in the UK. It was part of the sweeping welfare reform originally proposed in the *Beveridge Report on Social Insurance and Allied Services*. This proposed a system of state welfare that would provide support 'from the cradle to the grave'. It was to fight the five social evils of **want**, **disease**, **squalor**, **ignorance**, and **idleness**. A universal welfare state would provide a comprehensive health service, public housing, free and universal secondary education, and full employment, as well as welfare benefits to assist those in need.

> William Beveridge trained as a lawyer before the First World War, but served as an economist to advise Government on National Insurance and Old Age Pensions. He became director of the London School of Economics in 1919 and in 1941, he was asked by Ernest Bevin, a Government Minister, to conduct a review of the ways Britain should be rebuilt after the Second World War. His report, published in 1942, proposed a scheme of National Insurance, which gathered contributions from all working people and a system of health care provision and benefits to ensure a minimum standard of living for all. The proposals were adopted by the Attlee Government following the War. The NHS was established in 1948 and a system of social security provided security 'from cradle to the grave'.

The principles of the NHS were that the state was to take collective responsibility for a **universal and comprehensive range of health services** with equality of access for all.

The state took the responsibility to fund a centrally directed NHS from general taxation. It would remove inequalities in access and in the quality of health provision. The whole population would be entitled to the full range of health services free at the point of need. It would be responsible for improving the nation's health through education and prevention as well as for diagnosis and treatment. Health provision would be equal in every area and access would be equal irrespective of wealth.

The Acheson Report

The Acheson Report which was published in 1998 provided an analysis of the health of the UK. The proposals it made for addressing the problems it had highlighted became the basis of the Labour Government's policies towards health care. Its conclusions pointed to the strong relationship between social class and ill-health and its solutions centred on actions that would be targeted at the less well off in order to reduce the impact of poverty on health.

> *all policies likely to have a direct or indirect effect on health should be evaluated in terms of their impact on health inequalities, and should be formulated in such a way that by favouring the less well off they will, wherever possible, reduce such inequalities.*
>
> (Acheson Report 1998)

The report called for:

- an increase in benefit levels for women of childbearing age, expectant mothers, young children and older people.
- more funding for schools in deprived areas, better nutrition at schools and an emphasis on 'health promoting schools'.
- restrictions on smoking in public places, a ban on tobacco advertising and promotion, increases in the price of tobacco and provide nicotine replacement therapy on the NHS.

Recent government strategies for tackling health inequalities have tried to put the emphasis on structures and programmes aimed at prevention.

155

How might this boost my grade?

Developing your reading for information will help you ...

get the best information from textbooks and other materials given to you in class

not waste time gathering information that is not useful

be able to spot important points

cover a lot of background reading and get good examples

expand your vocabulary and improve your writing

get the best out of the written sources in Paper 2

NOTE TAKING

Candidates should be encouraged to read and make notes ... and spend some time on skills such as note taking and speed reading.

Higher Modern Studies Conditions and Arrangements

Developing this skill will help your knowledge and understanding because it will enable you to organise your notes for assessments and exam revision.

What should I write down when I take notes?

Taking notes is more than just copying. Your notes should be a clear summary of the important points. Do not just start taking notes as soon as you have a piece of text in front of you. When you take notes you must know exactly why you are taking them and what you are going to use them for.

How can I organise my notes to help me learn?

A two-column layout where you separate the main ideas from the details is a good way of organising your notes. The main ideas stand out and make them easier to revise.

For example, a two-column layout of notes might look like this:

EXAMPLE OF NOTE TAKING

TWO-COLUMN NOTE TAKING LAYOUT	
Turn titles, subheadings, topic sentences into questions or statements.	Write answers to the questions. Organise your ideas numerically and/or alphabetically. Use bullets, dashes, symbols, highlights, and abbreviations.
For example:	
What should I write down when I take notes?	Only write down IMPORTANT information. Look for: • Bold print, underlining, italics • Information in boxes, with icon or symbol • Headings and subheadings • Examples, details, quotes you could use in essay, assessment or exam • Information that –
Leave space to add notes and questions later.	Teacher emphasises – Book or text repeats – Might be in an assessment or the exam
How to take notes faster	1. Abbreviate familiar words/use symbols 2. Use bulleted lists, not full sentences 3. Cut unnecessary words 4. Use dramatic, headline sentences
Words to use when summarising:	Argues, asserts, concludes, considers, discusses, emphasises, examines, explores, focuses on, implies, mentions, notes, points out, says, states, suggests
At the end of your notes write a summary of the most important points and/or questions you still need to answer.	

You may also want to use patterned notes like spider diagrams, mind maps and other kinds of diagrams. Some people find patterns easier than lists of information and they can be useful for revision and planning essays and reports.

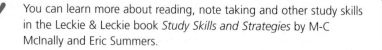 You can learn more about reading, note taking and other study skills in the Leckie & Leckie book *Study Skills and Strategies* by M-C McInally and Eric Summers.

How might this boost my grade?

Developing your note taking will help you ...

gather relevant information for assessments and examination

see the overall picture

keep up-to-date easily

be well organised for revision

plan well-structured essays and reports

KEEPING UP-TO-DATE

 Candidates require information and exemplification from the 21st century. Modern Studies is a dynamic subject.

Principal Assessor's Report

Examiners expect up-to-date information and examples in your essays and reports. The statistics and examples you use should be from the 21st century – i.e. after the year 2000!

As you study each theme be aware of changes in election results, leaders, policies, etc., and make sure you are not quoting out-of-date information.

What can I do to keep up-to-date?

Read a quality newspaper at least once a week. The Sunday editions and news magazines report the main events of the week in depth. Most quality newspapers have websites where you can read articles online. Some, like the *Scotsman*, have archives of back articles organised by topic.

It is a good idea to search news websites for current examples and keep a lookout for current affairs programmes and documentaries.

Keeping up-to-date does not have to take up a lot of your time. You can download weekly podcasts from news and current affairs websites and get news alerts by email, mobile or RSS.

You can access the sources below, and other Higher Modern Studies sources, at the Leckie & Leckie Learning Lab [http://www.leckieandleckie.co.uk/ learning_lab/free_resources/higher_modern_studies_weblinks.asp]

EXAMPLES OF SOURCES OF UP-TO-DATE INFORMATION FOR MODERN STUDIES

Scottish Daily Broadsheets	National Daily Broadsheets
The Herald The Scotsman Dundee Courier Press & Journal	The Daily Telegraph The Guardian The Independent The Times
Scottish Sunday Broadsheets	National Sunday Broadsheets
The Sunday Herald Scotland on Sunday	The Sunday Telegraph The Observer Independent on Sunday The Sunday Times
News Magazines	News Online
The Economist New Statesman Time Newsweek	BBC News Channel 4 News ITN Online SKY News CNN Al-Jazeera
National TV Programmes	Scottish TV Programmes
Panorama (BBC1) Question Time (BBC1) Newsnight (BBC2) Dispatches (Channel 4) Unreported World (Channel 4) Tonight (ITV)	Reporting Scotland (BBC1) The Politics Show (BBC1) Politics Now (ITV)
UK Parliament	Scottish Parliament
Parliament Live	Holyrood TV

This is a fairly long list, but do not panic – you do not have to use all the sources. Find a few good sources you like and use them to regularly update your notes.

How might this boost my grade?

Keeping up-to-date will help you ...

gain marks for current information and examples

improve your background knowledge

develop your Modern Studies vocabulary and writing style

ANALYSING AND EVALUATING

For an award at Grade A candidates should be able to ... demonstrate skills of analysis in a well balanced way, with relevant and detailed exemplification and by reaching relevant, well developed conclusion(s) ... demonstrate evaluating skills by a relevant, accurate and well-developed evaluation of complex sources.

Higher Modern Studies Conditions and Arrangements

Analysing and evaluating are two very important skills – they are your key to a good grade in Higher Modern Studies. Both skills require you to weigh up information and make a decision about its usefulness and accuracy.

The first step in analysing and evaluating is organising information and separating fact from opinion.

EXAMPLE OF SEPARATING FACT FROM OPINION

These newspaper articles about the 2007 Scottish Parliament election illustrate the difference between fact and opinion.

Article A

High number of spoiled papers puts spotlight on new system

VOTER confusion was blamed for a massive increase in the number of rejected ballot papers.

As many as 100,000 papers were rejected by returning officers - prompting calls for an urgent investigation.

The decision to hold three elections using three different voting systems on the same day also came in for severe criticism. The use of electronic vote counting for the first time also led to delays across the country, including Fife and East Kilbride.

Alex Salmond, the SNP leader, used his victory speech in Gordon to attack the voting system used.

He said the fact that thousands of votes went uncounted was "totally unacceptable in a democratic society". Turnout figures were also much lower than predicted - but that was at least in part due to the fact that spoiled papers do not count towards turnout. In Glasgow Anniesland, 1736 votes were rejected, while in Airdrie and Shotts the number of spoiled papers - 1536 - was bigger than the majority secured by Labour's Karen Whitefield.

The Herald, 4 May, 2007

FACTS
(Both articles)

1 There were as many as 100,000 spoiled ballot papers.
2 In some constituencies, number of spoiled ballot papers was more than the winning candidate's majority.
3 There was criticism of the new election system.

Article B

The biggest poll debacle in the history of British democracy sees up to one in ten votes thrown out

SCOTLAND'S status as a modern democracy was dealt a grievous blow yesterday by a scandal in which up to one in ten votes in the Holyrood election were thrown in the bin uncounted.

In a development that could bring into question the legitimacy of the Scottish Parliament poll; as many as 100,000 ballot papers were spoiled. That averages out as one in 20 votes but in some seats a tenth of the papers were spoiled.

In about one in six constituencies, the number of spoiled votes was bigger than the successful candidate's winning margin. They included Airdrie and Shotts, Livingston, Linlithgow, Stirling, Ochil, Govan, Central Fife, Dunfermline West and Cunninghame North.

At the root of the debacle were new, convoluted and potentially misleading election rules that lawyers say could expose the election results to an unprecedented legal challenge.

Politicians of all parties queued up to promise inquiries and to trade blame for the failures that resulted in the proportion of spoiled ballots rising from 0.8 per cent in the last Holyrood election in 2003 to about 5 per cent this time.

The Scotsman, 5 May, 2007

OPINIONS
(Article B)

A It was the biggest shambles in the history of British elections.
B Scotland's position as a democracy was called into question.
C The new election rules were to blame for the situation.

Both articles contain the same three main facts, but Article B also has comment. The writer gives an opinion that the new election rules for the Scottish Parliament resulted in an election fiasco that undermined Scottish democracy. It is up to the reader to judge whether the facts given in the article back up that opinion.

What is analysis?

In Modern Studies, analysis means showing balance by giving information on both sides of an argument and reaching a conclusion about what the information shows. To do this you must be able to give opinions and back them up with facts. You will use this skill throughout your Higher Modern Studies work, but it is particularly important for Paper 1 essays.

How do I show analysis?

Showing balance

Your first step is to show balance by giving both sides of an argument. Even if you agree with a certain point of view, or you think a particular opinion is the right one, in Modern Studies you always have to show an awareness of the opposing point of view. This is particularly important in your essays. The diagram below shows you the structure for a balanced essay.

A Balanced Essay

To what extent ... Assess ...
Discuss ... Examine ... Critically examine

1. Introduction setting out the answer
2. Main body giving ...

Arguments For
Strengths
Good points

Arguments Against
Weaknesses
Bad points

+ balanced comment on the issue in the question

3. Conclusion prioritising the main points

Reaching conclusions

A conclusion is the opinion or judgement you reach after looking at the evidence. In Modern Studies essays and reports you should come to two types of conclusion:

● a mini-conclusion, after a few main points, giving an opinion on what the information shows
● an overall conclusion about all the evidence you have presented

What is evaluating?

Evaluating is looking at information and judging its significance and worth. You will use this skill throughout your Higher Modern Studies work, but it is particularly important for the Paper 2 Decision Making Exercise.

How do I evaluate information?

Detecting bias

Bias means supporting only one opinion or view. Bias can be shown by:

● giving only one side of an argument and ignoring the opposing view
● providing only favourable facts about one view and only unfavourable facts about the other
● using exaggerated or mistaken information in support of a view – a very common form of bias found in the Paper 2 Decision Making Exercise

Synthesising

The examiners expect you to be able to synthesise information. This means putting information together from a number of different sources. What gets you high marks in Higher Modern Studies is being able to find the common thread and put information together in a way that answers the question. Paper 2 specifically tests you on this, but you also need to be able to synthesise information to argue your point in essays and to write notes that give you good information with relevant examples.

EXAMPLE OF SYNTHESIS

The following example about voter turnout shows you how to synthesise information from a number of sources.

Step 1

Using your reading for information skills you identify four important points from the *Higher Modern Studies Course Notes* and examples to back them up.

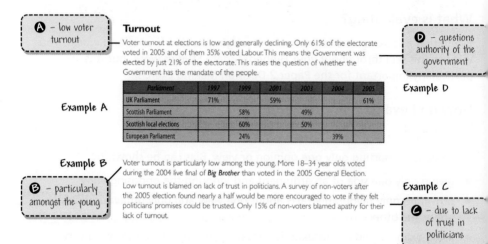

Ⓐ – low voter turnout

Ⓑ – particularly amongst the young

Example A

Example B

Turnout

Voter turnout at elections is low and generally declining. Only 61% of the electorate voted in 2005 and of them 35% voted Labour. This means the Government was elected by just 21% of the electorate. This raises the question of whether the Government has the mandate of the people.

Parliament	1997	1999	2001	2003	2004	2005
UK Parliament	71%		59%			61%
Scottish Parliament		58%		49%		
Scottish local elections		60%		50%		
European Parliament		24%			39%	

Voter turnout is particularly low among the young. More 18–34 year olds voted during the 2004 live final of **Big Brother** than voted in the 2005 General Election.

Low turnout is blamed on lack of trust in politicians. A survey of non-voters after the 2005 election found nearly a half would be more encouraged to vote if they felt politicians' promises could be trusted. Only 15% of non-voters blamed apathy for their lack of turnout.

Ⓓ – questions authority of the government

Example D

Example C

Ⓒ – due to lack of trust in politicians

Step 2

Using your data handling skills you add examples from the table to back this up.

Voter turnout is low.

For example, just over half the electorate voted in UK elections and around a third in elections for the European Parliament. Turnout fell dramatically from 71% in 1997 General Election to 59% in 2001. This pattern was repeated in elections for the Scottish Parliament where the turnout dropped from 60% in 1999 to 50% in 2003.

However, there has been a slight increase in turnout in recent years. In elections to the UK Parliament, turnout was up 3% to 61% in 2005.

Step 3

You realise you need to keep up-to-date. There was an election to the Scottish Parliament in 2007 and you want to see if this slight upward trend in turnout continued. You find this information online.

| bbc.co.uk | | | Home | TV | Radio | Talk | Where I Live | A-Z Index | | Search |

● **UK version** ● International version | About the versions   Low graphics | Accessibility help

BBC NEWS **Scottish elections 2007**

News Front Page
World
UK
England

Last Updated: Friday, 4 May, 2007, 17:10 GMT 18:10 UK

| Parliament A-Z | Constituency map | Regions map | Councils A-Z | Council map |

RESULTS AT A GLANCE

Party	LAB	SNP	LD	CON	GRN	OTH
Total	46	47	16	17	2	1

Turnout 2,016,978 51.8% +2.5%   EXAMPLE A

In 2007 Scottish Parliament election turnout was up 1·8% to 51·8%.

Turnout is particularly low amongst young people.

For example, more 18–34 year olds voted in 2004 Big Brother final than 2005 election.

Step 4

You also have the following table as a source and realise it gives you extra information.

Estimated turnout by population group, 2005 Based on a MORI Poll	
Total	**61%**
Age	
18-24 Example B	37%
25-34	48%
35-44	61%
45-54	64%
55-64	71%
65+	75%

Source: Election 2005: turnout – Electoral Commission Report, October 2005

Turnout for 18–34 year olds in the 2005 General Election was under 50% and for 18–24 year olds it was even lower at 37%.

Lack of trust in politicians, not apathy, blamed for low turnout.

In a survey after 2005 election only 15% claimed apathy as a reason for not voting.

Step 5

You also have information from the Power Inquiry about the level of lack of trust in politicians.

Power to the People

Surveys consistently display very low levels of trust in politicians at least since the early 1980s. These tend to find that those who say they trust politicians rarely rises above 25 per cent and usually hovers at just below 20 per cent ...   *Example C*

These findings remain true for the 2005 General Election. Power conducted its own survey of 1,025 people who were on the electoral register but did not cast their vote at that election... This showed that only 19 per cent cited apathy as a reason for not voting when asked the 'open' question: 'what was the main reason for you not voting on 5th May', 36 per cent of non-voters cited political reasons such as a lack of difference between the parties and claims that politicians 'could not be trusted'.   *Example C*

For example, the 'Power Inquiry' Report stated that in surveys since 1980s, the level of trust in politicians is around 20%.

In 'Power' Inquiry's own survey, 36% of voters gave political reasons like lack of trust or difference between politicians as there reason for not voting.

Low turnout means that the Government is elected by a small percentage of the electorate and this brings their authority into question.

Labour Government was elected by only 21% of total electorate.

Step 6

You know that the examiners like Scottish examples where appropriate and you decide to find out online if this also applies to elections in Scotland.

BBC NEWS | Election 2007 | Scottish Parliament | Election Result: Scotland

http://news.bbc.co.uk/1/shared/vote2007/scottish_parliment/html/scoreboard_99999.stm   ▼   ▶   G▾ Google

Getting Started   Latest Headlines   Microsoft Outlook W...   Microsoft Outlook W...   Integrated Catalogue ...   THE BRITISH LIBRAR...   PDQ Digital Media S

bbc.co.uk   Home TV Radio Talk Where I Live A-Z Index   [Search]

UK version International version | About the versions   Low graphics | Accessibility help

BBC NEWS

Scottish elections 2007

Last Updated: Friday, 4 May, 2007, 17:10 GMT 18:10 UK

News Front Page
World
UK
England
Northern Ireland
Scotland
Wales
Business
Politics
Health
Education
Science/Nature
Technology
Entertainment
Also in the news

Video and Audio

Have Your Say
Magazine
In Pictures
Country Profiles
Special Reports

RELATED BBC SITES

| Parliament A-Z | Constituency map | Regions map | Councils A-Z | Council map |

CONSTITUENCIES

Party	Seats	Net+/-	Votes	Votes%	+/-%
LAB	37	-9	648,374	32.2	-2.5
SNP	21	+12	664,227	32.9	+9.1
LD	11	-2	326,232	16.2	+0.9
CON	4	+1	334,743	16.6	-0.0

REGIONS

Party	Seats	Net+/-	Votes	Votes%	+/-%
SNP	26	+8	633,401	31.0	+10.2
CON	13	-2	284,005	13.9	-1.6
LAB	9	+5	595,415	29.2	-0.1
LD	5	+1	230,671	11.3	-0.5
GRN	2	-5	82,584	4.0	-2.8

SCOTTISH ELECTIONS 2007

SCOTTISH PARLIAMENT RESULTS

Party	Const	Regn	+/-	Tot
SNP	21	26	+20	47
LAB	37	9	-4	46
CON	4	13	-1	17
LD	11	5	-1	16
Others	0	3	-14	3

After 129 of 129 seats declared

WELSH ASSEMBLY ELECTIONS 2007
‣ Full coverage
ENGLISH COUNCIL ELECTIONS
‣ Local council coverage

KEY STORIES

Example D

Example D

The trend is similar in Scotland where the SNP got an average of 31·8% of the constituency and regional votes in 2007.

How might this boost my grade?

Developing analysis and evaluation will help you ...

put together a good set of notes using information from a variety of sources

provide a line of argument and provide balanced conclusions for your essays

find and connect information in the Decision Making Exercise and write a good report

DATA HANDLING

... candidates should be taught the data-handling required for Higher and be able to produce detailed descriptions and in-depth analysis.

Higher Modern Studies Conditions and Arrangements

Data handling is extracting and using information from charts, graphs, tables and maps. Most of your Modern Studies sources of information contain data that you need to evaluate and Paper 2 tests your ability to handle data.

What kind of data will I have to handle?

You are likely to handle two main types of data – time and comparison – presented in tables or graphics like bar graphs (charts), line graphs, pie charts and cartograms (maps).

How do I handle data?

You can use the mnemonic **DATA (Date, Amount, Trend, Accuracy)** to help you.

When presented with a set of data look for:

- Date – the time period covered, the time intervals between points in the data and the date of the source
- Amount – the unit of measurement (currency, percentage, index numbers, etc.)
- Trend – the changes over time and comparisons
- Accuracy – the reliability of the source, the method of collection and the possibility of bias or error

DATA

Date   – Time period, intervals, date of source
Amount – Unit of measurement
Trend   – Highs, lows, links, out of the ordinary
Accuracy – Reliability, bias or error

How do I evaluate data in tables?

EXAM EXAMPLE

This table is from 2002, Decision Making Exercise 2 and is about the cost and future consequences of free personal care for the elderly. Notice how the mnemonic, DATA, can be used to help you find the main information.

Date

❶ Table covers cost of personal care in UK from 1995 to 2051
From 1995 onwards figures are projected
No regular interval between data points
No date given for the source

Amount

Three units of measurement:
❷ Cost of present system and free personal care in £ billion
❸ % of GDP for present system and free personal care; **Key** tells us this is percentage of UK's wealth spent on personal care
❹ % increase in tax to provide free care

The financial effects of free personal care in the UK (projected after 1995) ❶	1995	2010	2021	2031	2051	
Cost of present care system (£ billion)	7·1	9·0	12·1	17·1	27·0	❺
Cost to provide free personal care (£ billion)	8·2	10·9	14·7	20·8	33·4	
% GDP spent on present care system	1·0	0·9	1·0	1·1	1·1	❻
% GDP for free personal care	1·2	1·1	1·2	1·3	1·4	
% increase in tax to provide free personal care	0·3	0·3	0·1	0·4	0·5	❼

❷ ❸ ❹ (row labels)

GDP = Gross Domestic Product, a measure of a country's wealth ❽

Trend

❺ Cost in £ billion of present system and free personal care over time; rate of increase; comparison of two systems
❻ % GDP of present system and free personal care over time; rate of increase; comparison of two systems
❼ % increase in tax for free personal care over time; rate of increase
❽ Look out for anomalies (things that go against the trend)

Accuracy

Source is not given, but since it is in the examination can assume the data is accurate

How do I write a data evaluation?

This data evaluation is weak.

The cost of the present care system was £7·1 billion in 1995. By 2010 it will rise to £9·0 billion, by 2021 £12·1 billion, 2031 £17·1 billion and 2051 £27·0 billion. The cost of providing free personal care would be £8·2 billion in 1995, £10·9 billion in 2010, £14·7 billion in 2021, £20·8 billion in 2031 and £33·4 billion in 2051.

The present system of care accounted for 1·0% of GDP in 1995 and will rise to 1·1% by 2051. However, the percentage of GDP spent on free personal care would increase from 1·2% in 1995, which would need a 0·3% increase in tax, to 1·4% in 2051 which would require a 0·5% increase in tax.

Why is this data evaluation weak?

This evaluation is weak because it simply goes from left to right describing things in the table. There is a slight attempt to pick out a trend but it is too little and too descriptive.

This is good data evaluation.

| Trend is identified |

Free personal care is likely to cost more to provide than the present system. It is projected that by 2051 providing free personal care will require a 0·5% tax increase, as well as £15·3 billion and 0·3% of GDP more than the present system.

| Ideas are grouped and data is recalculated to describe the trend |

| Another trend is identified |

The cost of free personal care is projected to rise at a faster rate than the cost of the present system.

By 2051, the cost of the present system is projected to treble to £27 billion a year, whereas, at £33 billion a year, the cost of free personal care will be four times the cost in 1995.

| Comparisons are made to show the trend |

| Yet another trend is identified |

The difference in cost and tax increase becomes more marked after 2021.

Up to 2021, % of GDP is projected to decline and then the amount of the UK's wealth spent on the present system will remain constant at 1995 level, but providing free personal care will lead to a steady increase to 1·4% of GDP by 2051. After a drop in % tax increase to 0·1% in 2021, a 400% rise to 0·5% is projected in the next 30 years.

| Anomalies are spotted and their effects on the trend explained |

Why is this data evaluation good?

This is good evaluation because it:

- picks out the main points
- groups similar ideas
- identifies trends
- recalculates data
- makes comparisons
- spots anomalies

Words to use when evaluating data

Words to describe a trend

Between ... and ...

From ... to ...

Fell, declined, dropped, decreased, sank, went down

Rose, went up, increased

Remained steady, unchanged, did not change, remained constant, remained stable, stabilised

Slightly, a little, a lot, sharply, suddenly, steeply, gradually, gently, steadily

Reached a peak, peaked, reached their highest level, fell to a low, sank to a low

Words to make a comparison

Compared with, equally, likewise, similarly, in the same way, however, whereas, but, yet, although, instead, alternatively, on the contrary

Half, quarter, one-third, two-thirds, one-fifth, one-tenth ...

Double, treble, quadruple, twice, three times, four times ...

Common mistakes to avoid when evaluating data

Because	As, since
Use at the end of the sentence when the reason is most important	Use at the beginning of sentence when the reason is already known or less important
The source does not support the view because the amount of health spending increased.	*Since the amount of health spending increased, the view is not supported by the source.*
	As the amount of health spending increased, the source does not support the view.

Compared to	Compared with
Similarities between things that are different	Show similarities and differences between two things
In the source, unemployment is compared to a disease affecting whole families in poorer areas.	*Compared with better off areas, unemployment is higher in poorer areas.*

Different from, different to
Use different from not different to
The American healthcare system is different from the one in the UK.

Fewer	Less
When it is plural	When what is singular
The source shows that there are fewer beds for the elderly.	*The source shows that less money is being spent on care for the elderly.*

How do I evaluate data in graphs?

There are four basic types of statistical graph: **bar graph (chart)**, **line graph**, **pie chart** and **cartogram**.

Extra things to look out for on graphs and maps:

- **scale** which tells you the unit of measurement and variables
- **key** (or legend) which gives you the meaning of any colours or symbols

How do I evaluate bar charts (graphs)?

EXAM EXAMPLE

This source is from 2001, Decision Making Exercise 2. It combines a bar chart with a table and covers health spending and life expectancy in selected developed countries. This is an illustration of how you could evaluate it.

Date
1 1997

Amount
2 % of GDP
3 Key explains that you can use statistics to show what % of country's wealth is spent on health
4 Key explains which part of bar gives % for public spending and for private spending
5 Number of years expected to live from birth

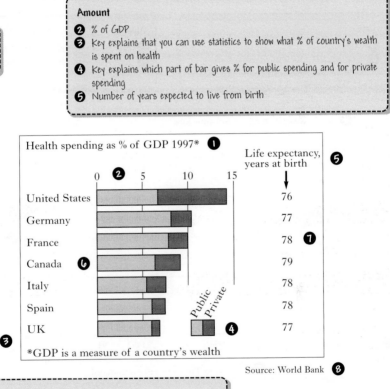

Health spending as % of GDP 1997*

Life expectancy, years at birth

*GDP is a measure of a country's wealth

Source: World Bank **8**

Trend
6 Each bar gives you three bits of information for comparison between the countries – total % of GDP spent on health care; % of GDP spent by the public sector on health care and % of total GDP spent by the private sector
7 Table allows you to compare life expectancy between the countries and look for links between health spending and life expectancy by comparing total spending, public spending and private spending with life expectancy

Accuracy
8 Source is given which allows you to judge reliability of the statistics. World Bank is a reputable source, so the figures are likely to be accurate

How do I evaluate line graphs?

Line graphs are good for showing a trend. You do not need to describe these graphs in detail, but you do need to pick out highs and lows and explain the trend.

EXAM EXAMPLE

This source is from 2005, Decision Making Exercise 1. It is two line graphs showing the impact of the EU Working Time Directive in the UK.

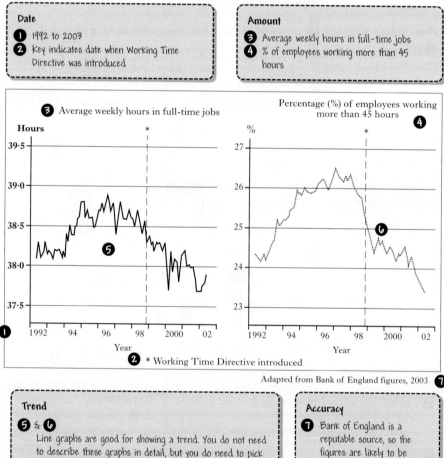

Date
① 1992 to 2003
② Key indicates date when Working Time Directive was introduced

Amount
③ Average weekly hours in full-time jobs
④ % of employees working more than 45 hours

③ Average weekly hours in full-time jobs

Percentage (%) of employees working more than 45 hours ④

② * Working Time Directive introduced

Adapted from Bank of England figures, 2003 ⑦

Trend
⑤ & ⑥
Line graphs are good for showing a trend. You do not need to describe these graphs in detail, but you do need to pick out highs and lows and explain the trend before and after the introduction of the Working Time Directive.
You can compare average weekly hours in full-time jobs before and after directive was introduced and percentage of employees working more than 45 hours before and after the directive was introduced. You can give an opinion about the effect of the introduction of Working Time Directive

Accuracy
⑦ Bank of England is a reputable source, so the figures are likely to be accurate. Year allows you to judge how up-to-date the figures are

How do I evaluate pie charts?

EXAM EXAMPLE

This is a source from 2005, Decision Making Exercise 2. The two pie charts show the results of a public opinion survey about the NHS.

Date

❶ Published in 2002 – no indication of when survey was carried out

Amount

❷ & ❸ % of those surveyed – no indication of how many people were surveyed; generally, the more people of different ages, gender and backgrounds, the more relevant the survey is

❹ Each segment represents % choosing that answer; key explains colour coding of the segments

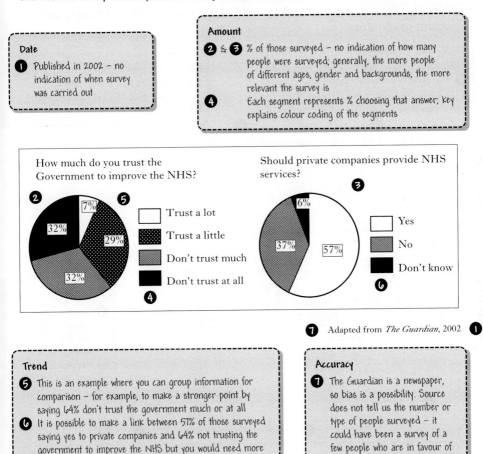

Adapted from *The Guardian*, 2002

Trend

❺ This is an example where you can group information for comparison – for example, to make a stronger point by saying 64% don't trust the government much or at all

❻ It is possible to make a link between 57% of those surveyed saying yes to private companies and 64% not trusting the government to improve the NHS but you would need more information to make this a definite link

Accuracy

❼ The Guardian is a newspaper, so bias is a possibility. Source does not tell us the number or type of people surveyed – it could have been a survey of a few people who are in favour of private health care

How do I evaluate cartograms?

EXAM EXAMPLE

This is a source from 2005, Decision Making Exercise 1. The cartogram shows the location of the selected countries and gives the statistical information in tables. Maps like this can also show information as bar or pie charts or colour coded regions or countries.

Date

❶ Map published in 2003 – date of individual statistics not given

Amount

❷ GDP per head in £
❸ Key explains GDP can be used as a measure of country's living standards
❹ % Unemployment rate

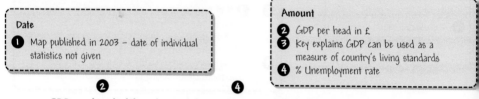

GDP per head* (£) and unemployment rates (%) in selected European countries

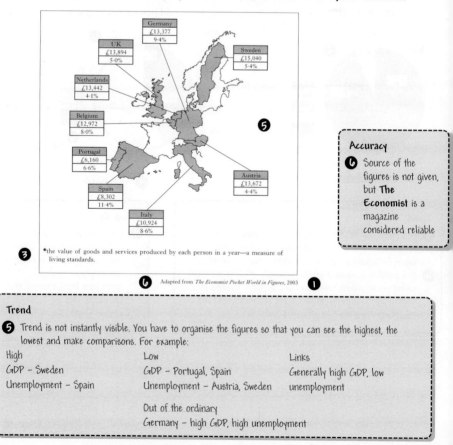

Accuracy

❻ Source of the figures is not given, but **The Economist** is a magazine considered reliable

❸ *the value of goods and services produced by each person in a year—a measure of living standards.

❻ Adapted from *The Economist Pocket World in Figures*, 2003   ❶

Trend

❺ Trend is not instantly visible. You have to organise the figures so that you can see the highest, the lowest and make comparisons. For example:

High	Low	Links
GDP – Sweden	GDP – Portugal, Spain	Generally high GDP, low
Unemployment – Spain	Unemployment – Austria, Sweden	unemployment
	Out of the ordinary	
	Germany – high GDP, high unemployment	

How might this boost my grade?

Developing your data handling will help you ...

understand data in textbooks and other sources

find good statistical examples for essays and reports

improve your speed in handling DME data

answer evaluating questions in Paper 2

find good statistical information for Paper 2 report

EFFECTIVE WRITING

Marks may be deducted for bad spelling and bad punctuation and for writing that is difficult to read.

Modern Studies Higher Examination Paper

In order to avoid losing marks, it is important to develop your writing skills and pay attention to the basics. Your grade depends on how clearly and accurately you write answers to the questions you are asked.

How can I improve my spelling?

Keep a dictionary with you and look up words. Practise spelling words you have a problem with. Beware of the spell check set to American English.

There is nothing more off putting to markers than the incorrect use of Modern Studies terms – make sure you learn to spell and use these correctly.

Common Modern Studies terms

alliance	environment	participation
ballot	exaggeration	president
benefit	exclusion	pressure
biased	executive	principal
bureaucracy	finance	principle
candidate	government	privilege
commission	Holyrood	professional
committee	immigration	proportional
consensus	inequality	rebuttal
constituency	influence	recommendation
council	institution	referendum
councillor	legislation	representation
decision	military	response
democracy	minister	scrutinise
development	nuclear	secretary
devolution	opinion	security
different	opposition	transferable
discrimination	parliament	Westminster

As you discover new words add them to your vocabulary list and practise using them in your essays and reports.

Common confusions to avoid

Affect	Effect
To cause or influence; usually a verb	Result or consequence; usually a noun
Bad weather on polling day can affect turnout.	*An effect of bad weather on polling day is low turnout.*

Practice	Practise
Training, rehearsal; is a noun	To prepare, try out; is a verb
It is a good idea to get some exam practice.	*It is a good idea to practise for the exam.*

Principle	Principal
Belief, standard, attitude or opinion; is a noun	Main, chief or most important; usually an adjective
Collectivism is a founding principle of the Welfare State.	*One of the principal reasons for changes to the welfare system is the increasing cost of providing support.*

Their	There
Belonging to	Place or position
Political parties should connect more closely with their voters.	*There are political parties that connect closely with voters.*

They're*
Short for *they are*
They're the political party that connects most closely with voters.

* *Do not use an abbreviation in an essay or report unless it is a quotation in speech marks*

How can I improve my punctuation?

Learn to use punctuation marks correctly. A badly punctuated essay or report creates a very bad impression on the marker. It is worth taking time to get your punctuation correct.

If you have problems punctuating your written work, it is a good idea to keep a table like this beside you when you are writing notes, essays and reports.

' apostrophe	To show possession of (or belonging to) or shorten words
Capital letters	To show start of a sentence and proper nouns – names of people and places even when abbreviated
: colon	To introduce – lists, explanations or quotations
, comma	To separate items in a list or mark off words and phrases in sentences to make the meaning clear
☠ *Beware of the comma splice* – see opposite for how to avoid this mistake!	
- dash	To show an afterthought or instead of a colon
! exclamation mark	To show surprise, warning or other emotion
. full stop	To show end of a sentence
" " or ' ' **inverted commas**	Speech marks to show words said or quotation or to show title of books, newspapers, magazines, programmes, etc.
parenthesis	Brackets ( ) or commas , , or dashes - - to separate additional information
? question mark	To ask for information or rhetorical question which only requires reader to think about the answer
; semi-colon	To connect two ideas that could be separate sentences or to separate items in lists where commas are already used
... three dots	At end of sentence to show sudden break off or in middle of sentence to show words are missed out
☠ *Warning* – do not shorten quotations from the sources in Paper 2	

How to avoid the comma splice

The comma splice – joining two separate parts of sentence with a comma – is one of the most common punctuation mistakes. It is worth learning how to avoid it because making this mistake can lose you marks.

Here is an example of the type of comma splice mistake which is often made in Modern Studies essays.

> There are many things that influence voting behaviour, social class is one of the most important.

Two points are being made – one about voting behaviour and one about social class. They are not part of a list. They are completely separate and therefore cannot be artificially joined by a comma.

To correct this comma splice you have to show the separation between the two points. You can do this by:

- Using separate sentences
  > There are many things that influence voting behaviour. Social class is one of the most important.

- Using a semi-colon
  > There are many things that influence voting behaviour; social class is one of the most important.

- Joining with a conjunction (for example and, but, or, because, since)
  > There are many things that influence voting behaviour and social class is one of the most important.

☠ **Warning!**
However, moreover, then – are NOT conjunctions.

With these words, use a semi-colon or start a new sentence.

> There are many things that influence voting behaviour. However, social class is one of the most important.

How can I improve my writing?

- Develop a good structure and writing style for your essays and reports.
- Group your information into proper sentences and paragraphs.
- Make each paragraph about the same topic or point.
- Make your point clear in the first sentence.
- Explain your point and give examples in the rest of the paragraph.
- Begin each paragraph on a new line.
- Link your paragraphs to each other and to your line of thought.

Linking words to use when writing essays and reports

It is a good idea to learn and practise linking. For example:

Introducing information	Emphasising
Firstly, secondly, thirdly, then, next, eventually, subsequently, at last, in the end, afterwards, finally, in addition, moreover, furthermore	*In particular, specifically, significantly, more important, notably, clearly, above all, in fact, indeed, not only … but also*
Making points	**Comparing**
Therefore, thus, as a result, accordingly, because, as, hence, so, consequently, until, as long as, whenever	*Compared with, compared to, in the same way, as with, equivalent, equally, likewise, similarly*
Giving examples	**Changing position**
For example, such as, for instance, as illustrated by, to show that, in the case of, evidence such as	*But, however, on the other hand, nevertheless, still, alternatively, although, despite this, whereas, on the contrary, instead, the opposite*
Giving opinions	**Summing up**
Suggest, conclude, deduce, it would seem, infer, imply, consider, propose, the fact that, when facts such as … are considered	*To conclude, to sum up, in summary, overall, on the whole, throughout, in the end, finally, throughout*

How might this boost my grade?

Learning to write effectively will help you …

impress markers with your writing style

avoid basic errors in spelling or punctuation

clearly express your point of view

write fluent, well-balanced essays

write clear, well-structured reports

 The next two chapters show you how you use these skills to write essays, answer evaluating questions and write reports.

Glossary

GLOSSARY

Analysis – A detailed examination of information

Anomaly – A result that deviates from the expected

Balance – A presentation of both sides of an argument

Bar graph – Statistical information displayed using bars

Bias – Only one side of an argument given

Cartogram – A map with statistical information

Cite – Quote/use information from a specific source

Comment – Make a statement about a particular issue

Comparison data – Statistics that can be weighed against each other

Conclusion – A statement about a pattern or a trend that can be discerned

Data – Information that is given as values or measurements

Data evaluation – Assessing the usefulness of statistics

Data handling – Identifying and using information from bar charts, maps, graphs, etc.

Emphasis – Stress placed to reinforce importance

Evaluating – Judging the value or importance

Exaggeration – Over emphasising importance/lack of importance

Exemplification – Giving an example/providing more depth

Fact – A piece of information that is true and verified as such

Key – A list of symbols/wording used on a graph or map

Knowledge and understanding – Information learned

Legend – A list of symbols/wording used on a graph or map

Line graph – Statistical information displayed by lines

Mnemonic – A form of words or letters that makes information easier to remember

Open question – A question that cannot simply be answered by saying 'yes' or 'no'

Opinion – A personal view on an issue. This may, or may not, be based on fact.

Pie chart – Statistical information displayed in a circular chart

Podcast – Digital media file – internet streamed information

Preview – Have a quick look at information

Read actively – Read with a purpose

Reading aids – Highlighted information within text, perhaps in the form of emboldened words or italics

Recall – Remembered information

RSS – News feed from a website

Scale – Measurement used on a map

Synthesis – Combining ideas and information

Time data – Statistics that show information over a period of time

Time period – Time intervals between points/time period covered by data

Trend – A pattern, or tendency, that can be identified

Unit of quantity – Measurement used in statistical data, e.g. currency, percentage, etc.

2 Paper 1

INTRODUCTION TO PAPER 1

To pass, responses will need to feature developed knowledge and understanding, relevant contemporary exemplification and balanced analysis.

Principal Assessor's Report

Paper 1 has three sections containing the choices for your essay questions.

What skills do I need for Paper 1?

You need good notes with up-to-date examples to show your knowledge and understanding. You need analysis to give both sides of an issue and come to a balanced conclusion. You also need good essay writing skills because you have to put all this together (synthesise it) in a well-written, well-argued essay.

Look at Chapter 1 if you need to brush up on any of these skills!

What topics does Paper 1 cover?

Paper 1 is divided into three sections; each question covers a different study theme as follows:

Section A - *Political Issues in the United Kingdom*	
Question A1:	Devolved Decision Making in Scotland
Question A2:	Decision Making in Central Government
Question A3:	Political Parties and their Policies
Question A4:	Electoral Systems, Voting and Political Attitudes

Section B – *Social Issues in the United Kingdom*	
Question B5:	Wealth and Health Inequalities in the United Kingdom
Question B6:	Wealth and Health Inequalities in the United Kingdom

Section C - *International Issues*	
Question C7:	The Republic of South Africa
Question C8:	The People's Republic of China
Question C9:	The United States of America
Question C10:	The European Union
Question C11:	The Politics of Development in Africa
Question C12:	Global Security

Make sure you know the question number of the study themes you have covered.

Remember, you have to choose from two questions in Wealth and Health Inequalities in the United Kingdom.

What do I have to do?

The front of the paper will have instructions like this.

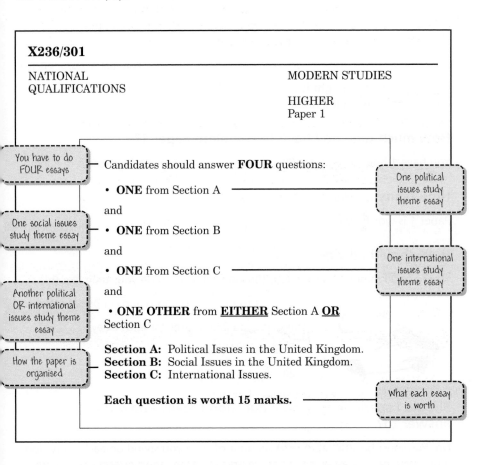

Make sure you know what you have to do before you start the paper.

Should I do my two essays from the one section first?

No. You need a good balance between your political, social and international answers so you pick up marks in each of them. It is better to complete an essay in each of the sections before deciding whether you will do another Section A or Section C question for your fourth essay.

Be careful not to think of your fourth essay as an 'extra'. Think carefully about your choice and spend as much time on it as you did on your other essays.

TIMING

A significant number of candidates either made no, or at best a token attempt, to answer a fourth question … candidates should be aware of the importance of time management.

Principal Assessor's Report

Getting your timing right is vital in Paper 1. You must give equal time to each essay to achieve a good grade.

How much time do I have to complete Paper 1?

You have 1 hour 30 minutes (90 minutes) to complete the four essays in Paper 1.

How many marks is Paper 1 worth?

Paper 1 is worth 60 marks – each essay is worth 15 marks.

How should I divide my time?

You have 90 minutes to complete the paper. Try to divide your time like this:

2 minutes to read instructions and choose questions.

This gives you 22 minutes for **each** essay:

– 2 minutes to plan

– 20 minutes to write

Should I spend longer on a question I really know the answer to?

No. You must be strict about the amount of time you spend on each essay. Too much time on one essay is time and marks lost from another essay. If you are rushing your last essays you are unlikely to be heading towards a good mark. You need four equally well-structured and well-argued essays. You have to organise your time so that all your essays achieve a good pass.

Should I skip planning my essay?

No. It is worth taking a couple of minutes to plan your answer. It does not have to be anything elaborate – just a few notes to give your essay a structure. Without an essay plan you are likely to wander off topic and lose time and marks.

THE ESSAY STRUCTURE

... numbering and bullet points are not acceptable in Paper 1.

Principal Assessor's Report

How do I structure an essay?

Your essay needs a basic structure for you to build up your ideas. There are certain basic ingredients for a successful essay.

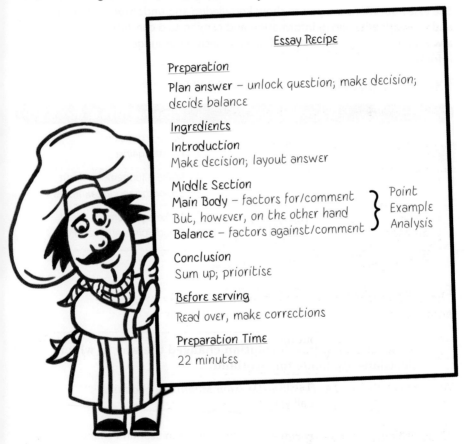

Essay Recipe

Preparation
Plan answer – unlock question; make decision; decide balance

Ingredients
Introduction
Make decision; layout answer

Middle Section
Main Body – factors for/comment   } Point
But, however, on the other hand   } Example
Balance – factors against/comment   } Analysis

Conclusion
Sum up; prioritise

Before serving
Read over, make corrections

Preparation Time
22 minutes

As you become more confident your essay recipe will become more adventurous. Your essay needs to flow in a logical manner to allow the examiner to follow your ideas.

THE ESSAY QUESTIONS

There is a continuing need to teach candidates how to respond to the wording of questions … they must be familiar with the implications of the different styles.

Principal Assessor's Report

What types of essay questions will I be asked?

The essay questions ask you to show knowledge and understanding, analysis and evaluation by giving information and coming to a conclusion. You will **always** have to show balance and make a decision or judgement about the information you put in your essay.

The type of question tells you what you have to do. For example:

Question	Meaning	What you have to do
To what extent *Assess*	How much?	Make a decision *For or Against*
Discuss	How accurate?	Make a judgement about *Strengths and Weaknesses*
Examine *Critically examine*	How good?	Make a judgement about *Good Points and Bad Points*

Examples of Paper 1 essay questions

Political Issues in the United Kingdom questions

> **To what extent has devolution changed the way in which decisions are made for Scotland?**
>
> *Study Theme 1A: Devolved Decision Making in Scotland*

This question asks: *How much* has decision making in Scotland changed since devolution?

> **Critically examine the view that pressure groups are a threat to democracy.**
>
> *Study Theme 1B: Decision Making in Central Government*

This question asks: *How good* is the view that pressure groups are a threat to democracy?

> **Assess the importance of party unity in achieving electoral success.**
>
> *Study Theme 1C: Political Parties and their Policies*

This question asks: *How much* has party unity to do with electoral success?

> ***There are fairer electoral systems than First Past the Post. Discuss.***
>
> *Study Theme 1D: Electoral Systems, Voting and Political Attitudes*

This question asks: *How accurate* is the claim that there are fairer systems than First Past the Post?

Social Issues in the United Kingdom questions

> **To what extent is there a link between income and health?**
>
> *Study Theme 2: Wealth and Health Inequalities in the United Kingdom*

This question asks: *How much* of a link is there between income and health?

> **Assess the effectiveness of government policies to tackle poverty.**
>
> *Study Theme 2: Wealth and Health Inequalities in the United Kingdom*

The question asked: *How much* of an effect have government policies had on poverty?

> ***Governments have done little to improve the social and economic position of ethnic minorities in the UK. Discuss.***
>
> *Study Theme 2: Wealth and Health Inequalities in the United Kingdom*

This question asks: *How accurate* is the claim that UK governments have not done a lot to improve the social and economic position of ethnic minorities?

> **Examine the claim that the UK has become a more equal society.**
>
> *Study Theme 2: Wealth and Health Inequalities in the United Kingdom*

This question asks: *How good* is the claim that UK is now a more equal society?

> **Critically examine the success of recent government measures to reduce gender inequalities.**
>
> *Study Theme 2: Wealth and Health Inequalities in the United Kingdom*

This question asks: *How good* have recent government measures been at reducing gender inequalities?

International Issues questions

> **To what extent is there still social and economic inequality in South Africa?**
>
> *Study Theme 3A: The Republic of South Africa*

This question asks: *How much* social and economic inequality still exists in South Africa?

> **The Communist Party may encourage social reform, but continues to discourage any political reform.**
> **Discuss.**
>
> *Study Theme 3B: The People's Republic of China*

This question asks: *How accurate* is the claim that the Communist Party encourages social reform but not political reform?

> **Assess the effectiveness of government policies to reduce economic and social inequalities.**
>
> *Study Theme 3C: The United States of America*

This question asks: *How much* of an effect have US government policies had on reducing economic and social inequalities?

> **Examine the decision making processes of the European Union.**
>
> *Study Theme 3D: The European Union*

This question asks: *How good* are the decision making processes of the European Union?

> **With reference to specific African countries (excluding the Republic of South Africa):**
> **Government domestic policies have been the main obstacles to economic and social development.**
> **Discuss.**
>
> *Study Theme 3E: The Politics of Development in Africa*

This question asks: *How accurate* is the claim that the domestic policies of the governments of African countries are the main things holding back development?

> **Critically examine the peacekeeping role of the United Nations.**
>
> *Study Theme 3F: Global Security*

This question asks: How good is the peace keeping role of the United Nations?

> !!!
>
> You can be asked any type of question in any study theme, but if you unlock the question you will understand the decision you have to make.

WRITING AN ESSAY

Candidates need to respond to the different styles and vocabulary of questions … give a well-developed, balanced answer and use recent exemplification.

Principal Assessor's Report

To get a good grade in a Higher Modern Studies essay you must demonstrate two main things:

- Knowledge and understanding – by giving good descriptions and examples
- Analysis – by giving different points of view, explaining causes and factors and reaching a balanced conclusion

In order to do this in **20 minutes** you need a good essay structure and a fluent writing style. All your essays should have a beginning – an introduction; a middle – a main body; and an end – a conclusion.

PLANNING

Some candidates have difficulty in addressing the question; often seeming to try to fit a learned response into the given question … candidates should focus on answering the question exactly as worded.

Principal Assessor's Report

You should always plan your essay so that it has balance.

What is 'balance'?

Balance is analysing the information on **both** sides of an issue and coming to a conclusion. In your Modern Studies essays you must **always** give the opposing view.

How do I show balance?

You show balance by unlocking the question, making your decision, giving **and** commenting on arguments for and against your decision.

Here is an example of how to plan a balanced answer for a 'to what extent' question.

EXAM EXAMPLE 1

> **To what extent has devolution changed the way in which decisions are made for Scotland?**
>
> *Study Theme 1A: Devolved Decision Making in Scotland*

1. Unlock the question

How much has decision making in Scotland changed since devolution?

2. Make your decision

Decision making in Scotland has changed significantly since devolution.

3. Find your balance

For	BUT	Against
Devolved powers		Reserved powers
Effects of AMS		Westminster system – Scotland Office, Secretary, MPs
Scottish Parliament – accountability, equality		
Scottish Government – power sharing		Demand for independence/more devolution

Analyse/comment on how much decision making has changed since devolution

This example may not be one of your study themes, but the steps – unlock the question, make your decision and find your balance – are the same for 'to what extent' and 'assess' questions in all study themes.

Here is an example of how to plan a balanced answer for a 'discuss' question.

EXAM EXAMPLE 2

> ***There are fairer electoral systems than First Past the Post. Discuss.***
>
> *Study Theme 1D: Electoral Systems, Voting and Political Attitudes*

1. Unlock the question
How accurate is the claim that there are fairer systems than First Past the Post?

2. Make your decision
PR systems are fairer to a certain degree.

3. Find your balance

Strengths	BUT	Weaknesses
PR systems –		PR systems -
Closer link between votes and seats		Break link between constituency and MP
More voter choice		Lack voter choice in candidate lists
Greater representation for smaller parties		Smaller parties undue influence in coalitions
Less tactical or wasted votes		Two chances to be elected
More consensus style government		Compromises no one voted for

Analyse/comment on whether there are fairer systems than First Past the Post

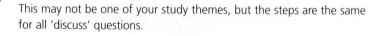

This may not be one of your study themes, but the steps are the same for all 'discuss' questions.

Here is an example of how to plan a balanced answer for a 'critically examine' question.

EXAM EXAMPLE 3

> **Critically examine the effectiveness of Congress and the Supreme Court in limiting the powers of the President.**
>
> *Study Theme 3C: The United States of America*

1. Unlock the question

How good are Congress and the Supreme Court at limiting the powers of the President?

2. Make your decision

Congress and the Supreme Court can limit the powers of the President only to a certain extent.

3. Find your balance

<u>Good Points</u>	BUT	<u>Bad Points</u>
Congress/Supreme Court can be effective because:		Checks and balances now less effective – President has become most powerful branch of government because:
Constitution		
Separation of Powers		Veto, Executive Orders
Checks and Balances –		Patronage – appointments, federal spending, popularity
Congress = law making, tax raising, approve appointments, impeachment, system of elections		Commander in Chief – national security, post-9/11, homeland security, Patriot Act
Supreme Court = judicial review - unconstitutional, judges appointed for life		

Analyse/comment on whether Congress and Supreme Court can limit the President

This may not be one of your study themes, but the steps are the same for all 'critically examine' and 'examine' questions.

WRITING AN INTRODUCTION

Some candidates waste precious time and sacrifice style by rewriting the question or writing over-lengthy introductions.

Principal Assessor's Report

How do I write an introduction?

Your introduction must unlock the question and show you understand the decision or judgement you have to make. You must also show how you intend to answer the question.

Here are examples of introductions to a 'to what extent' question.

EXAM EXAMPLE 1

> **To what extent has devolution changed the way in which decisions are made for Scotland?**
>
> *Study Theme 1A: Devolved Decision Making in Scotland*

This introduction is weak.

Devolution is the process by which power is handed down from Westminster to Holyrood. New Labour promised the Scottish electorate a referendum on having a Scottish Parliament with tax varying powers. The referendum showed an overwhelming desire to have a Scottish Parliament.

Why is this introduction weak?

This introduction is weak because it does not mention the decision that has to be made. There is no reference to a link between devolution and decision making. The writer has fallen into the trap of using the first lines of their notes as an introduction, without making sure they link directly to the question. The introduction does not show the marker how the question will be answered. It therefore serves no purpose and would receive no marks.

This is a better introduction, but it still has some flaws.

Devolution has, to some extent, changed the way in which decisions are made for Scotland. In 1999, the first elected Scottish Parliament met in Edinburgh. The main principles of the parliament are power sharing, accountability, accessibility and equal opportunities. These principles have influenced the way decisions are made in Scotland. This essay aims to illustrate the changes in decision making as a result of devolution.

Why is this introduction better?

This introduction is better because it shows an awareness of the decision to be made about the link between devolution and decision making. It lists some of the factors that will be developed in the essay.

What flaws does this introduction have?

The writer has not remembered that balanced comment and analysis are necessary in a Higher Modern Studies essay and has not referred to the other side of the argument. Also, the last sentence serves no purpose because the marker knows what the essay is about.

This introduction is much better.

The way decisions are made in Scotland has changed significantly as a result of devolution. In devolved matters, the Additional Member System of election produces a different kind of Scottish Parliament and Government with more power sharing, accountability, equality and openness. However, in reserved matters, the decision making processes of Westminster still apply. This illustrates that not all the decision making processes in Scotland have changed.

Why is this introduction much better?

This is a very good introduction because it links to the question and immediately states the decision that has been made. It clearly shows where the essay is going by listing the points that will be developed. It shows balance by referring to both sides of the argument and provides a conclusion. It is fluently written and does more than just reword the question.

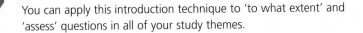

You can apply this introduction technique to 'to what extent' and 'assess' questions in all of your study themes.

Here are some examples of introductions to an 'examine' question.

EXAM EXAMPLE 2

> **Examine the link between income and health.**
>
> *Study Theme 2: Wealth and Health Inequalities in the United Kingdom*

This introduction is weak.

There is a health divide in Scotland between the rich and the poor. People in the richest postcodes have better health statistics than people in the poorest postcodes.

Why is this introduction weak?

This introduction is weak because it does not mention the decision that has to be made. There is no reference to how good the link is between income and health. It is very common for the first lines of notes to be used as an introduction and for no attempt to be made to link them to the question. The introduction does not show the marker how the question will be answered. It therefore serves no purpose and would receive no marks.

This is a better introduction, but it still has some flaws.

There is a link between income and health. Poor health can be caused by poverty, unhealthy lifestyle, diet and poor access to health care. All of these are the result of low income. This essay will show the extent of the link between income and health.

Why is this introduction better?

This introduction is better because it shows an awareness of the decision to be made about the link between income and health. It lists some of the factors that will be developed in the essay.

What flaws does this introduction have?

The writer does not say how much of a link there is between income and health. The introduction does not show balance because the other side of the argument has not been presented. Also, the last sentence serves no purpose because the marker already knows what is intended.

This introduction is much better.

There is a significant link between income and health. Factors connected with poor health such as poverty, lower social class, unemployment, unhealthy lifestyle and bad diet are all linked to low income. However, there are exceptions. Some individuals from higher socio-economic backgrounds also suffer from poor health as a result of poor lifestyle choices or genetics. This illustrates that income is not the only factor to impact on a person's health.

Why is this introduction much better?

This is a very good introduction because it links to the question and states the decision that has been made. It clearly shows where the essay is going by listing the points that will be developed. The marker is immediately alerted to the fact that this is a well-planned, well-structured essay. The introduction also shows balance by referring to both sides of the argument and providing a conclusion.

You can apply this introduction technique to 'examine' and 'critically examine' questions in all of your study themes.

Here is an example of an introduction to a 'discuss' question.

EXAM EXAMPLE 3

> **Immigration is an issue over which public opinion in the USA is divided.**
> **Discuss.**
>
> *Study Theme 3C: The United States of America*

As the previous examples show, an introduction should always convince the marker that the writer understands the question and knows the direction the essay will take.

In your introduction you must:

- Make a decision about the issue.
- Show a link to the question.
- Set out how the question will be answered.

Here is a very good introduction.

Immigration is an issue over which there is a deep division **1** of public opinion in the USA. **2** Both sides of the divide use economic, social and national security arguments to justify their point of view. Restrictionists see immigration, particularly illegal immigration, as a problem and want tougher controls, whereas liberalisers see benefits in immigration and want to legalise the position of illegal immigrants. **3**

Why is this a very good introduction?

This introduction fulfils all the criteria. It immediately gives a decision that the divide in public opinion is 'deep'. **1** It shows a link by using wording from the question and sets out how the question will be answered. It does this by briefly giving the position of the two sides of the divide in public opinion. **2** It states that both sides of the economic, social and national security arguments will be developed in the essay. **3** After reading this introduction the marker knows the writer fully understands the question and topic. The marker also knows that the writer is going to develop relevant points in a logical order to justify the conclusion that there is a deep division in American public opinion over the issue of immigration.

You can apply this introduction technique to 'discuss' questions in all of your study themes.

WRITING A MIDDLE SECTION

It is essential that information is constantly updated ... candidates are disadvantaged when they do not use recent exemplification ... Candidates should be encouraged to recall statistics correctly or not use them at all.

Principal Assessor's Report

The middle section of your essay is where you show your knowledge and understanding, balance and analysis.

The main body of your essay should have:

- a topic sentence at the start of each paragraph pointing out what the paragraph is about

- analysis of the main point of the paragraph
- accurate, detailed descriptions and/or examples in each paragraph
- a clear link between the information in the paragraph and the question
- links between each paragraph
- both sides of the argument
- balanced comment on the issue being discussed

How do I write a paragraph?

P	Point	– **sentence** giving **point of view** in response to the question
E	Example	– **illustrating** your point
A	Analysis	– **explain** what your point and example show
		– **expand** to show how your point fits into your line of argument
		– **link** by providing a mini-conclusion and moving to the next point

PEA — Point, Example, Analysis / Explain, Expand, Link

Here is an example of a paragraph developed using PEA.

EXAM EXAMPLE 1

> *There are fairer electoral systems than First Past the Post.*
> **Discuss.**
>
> *Study Theme 1D: Electoral Systems, Voting and Political Attitudes*

This paragraph is weak.

P Proportional Representation (PR) systems, such as the Additional Member System (AMS) used to elect the Scottish Parliament, are said to be fairer than First Past the Post because they result in a closer link between the number of votes a party receives and the number of seats it gets. E For example, in the 2007 elections to the Scottish Parliament, the party with the biggest number of MSPs – the Scottish National Party

– obtained an average of 32% of the votes in the constituency and regional list elections and gained 36% of the seats in the Scottish Parliament, whereas in the 2005 General Election the party with the most MPs – the Labour Party – got 35% of the votes but gained 55% of the seats in the House of Commons.

Why is this paragraph weak?

This paragraph is weak because although it makes a valid point and provides a good example it has no analysis.

How do I analyse?

You analyse by explaining, expanding and linking to the question. Each paragraph in your essay should contain a point of view, or opinion, about the question. Explaining means showing how your example illustrates your point of view. You expand by providing additional information to support your opinion. In each paragraph you should link back to the question to make sure that the information you have included is relevant. It is also important to link forward to your next paragraph so that you have a fluent, flowing style. The following two paragraphs demonstrate this technique.

This paragraph shows analysis, but it has some flaws.

P One of the criticisms of First Past the Post is that there is often a considerable discrepancy between the number of votes the winning party receives and the number of seats it gets. **E** For example, in the 2005 General Election the Labour Party got 35% of the votes and 55% of the seats in the House of Commons. **A – explain** This unfairness is further demonstrated by the fact that the simple majority, 'winner takes all' rule of First Past the Post resulted in the Labour Party forming a government with an overall majority of 66 seats despite only gaining just over one-third of the votes cast. **A – expand** A similar discrepancy exists in the constituency vote for the Scottish Parliament, where the SNP actually received more votes than the Labour Party but only gained 21 seats compared with Labour's 37. The difference is that the AMS used to elect the Scottish Parliament is a PR system designed to iron out this inconsistency in the first vote for regional list MSPs. As a result, the SNP formed a minority Scottish Government with 32% of the votes and 36% of the seats in the Scottish Parliament.

What flaws does this paragraph have?

Although this paragraph highlights a relevant point, which it develops with appropriate examples, it does not link. This paragraph needs more explicit linkage between the point made and the question asked. As it stands this paragraph is not specific enough. It lacks the purpose that a clear link to the question would give it.

> !!
> !.
> When you are learning how to write essays, marking where your point, example and different types of analysis begin is a good way of making sure you fully develop your paragraph. When you are more practised at essay writing you will no longer need this aid – and your paragraphs will flow naturally.

This paragraph is much better.

P One of the claims made for Proportional Representation (PR) systems, like the Additional Member System (AMS) used for elections to the Scottish Parliament, is that they are fairer than First Past the Post because they more truly reflect the wishes of the electorate. **E** For example, with the First Past the Post system smaller parties are under-represented because they receive more votes than seats, whereas the opposite is true for larger parties. This imbalance was amply demonstrated in the 2005 General Election where the Liberal Democrats won over one-fifth of the votes (22%) but less than one-tenth (9.6%) of the seats in the House of Commons. In comparison, the over-representation of the Labour Party, who received just over one-third (35%) of the votes and over half (55%) of the seats, was apparent. **A – explain** This shows that the simple majority, 'winner takes all' rule of the First Past the Post system, which resulted in Labour forming a majority government despite only 21% of the total electorate voting for them, has an inbuilt unfairness. **A – expand** Furthermore, this is in sharp contrast to the AMS used for the 2007 elections for the Scottish Parliament. In this case, the imbalance in the First Past the Post constituency vote, where the Scottish National Party (SNP) won more votes but fewer seats than Labour, was corrected in the proportional representation regional list vote. The SNP eventually won 32% of the votes and 35% of the seats. **A – link** This was a much fairer result because, unlike the outcome with First Past the Post, it truly reflected the wishes of the voters as demonstrated at the ballot box.

Why is this paragraph much better?

This paragraph shows explicit linkage between the point made and the question asked. It contains extensive information that is directly linked to the question and it has accurate and detailed examples. It discusses the issue raised in the question and comes to a sub-conclusion.

How do I write a fully developed paragraph?

You may be worried that you might not be able to write a fully developed paragraph. However, practising building a paragraph with PEA will improve your essay style. The following example shows you how to construct a paragraph.

EXAM EXAMPLE 2

> **To what extent are the founding principles of the welfare state being met?**
>
> *Study Theme 2: Wealth and Health Inequalities in the United Kingdom*

Step 1

Unlocking the question is your starting point for writing a fully developed paragraph. This question asks you to consider how much the welfare state's founding principles have changed. You decide that Beveridge's collectivist, universal, non-means tested approach to tackling the 'five giants' of want, disease, idleness, ignorance and squalor has changed significantly. You outline this line of argument in your introduction and decide that you will assess it by showing how each of the 'five giants' – poverty, ill health, unemployment, lack of education and poor housing – has changed.

Step 2

The key to a fully developed paragraph is your opening sentence.

This is a weak opening sentence.

 Pension Credit and Income Support do not meet the founding principles of the welfare state because they are means tested and not universal.

Why is this opening sentence weak?

The point being made is too narrow and specific. It comes to a conclusion at the start of the paragraph and this leaves no room for development. The most that can be added is a simple, factual example. Your opening sentence must give you scope for further analysis.

This is a better opening sentence.

 The welfare state's founding principle of tackling poverty ('want') through a universal, flat rate, contributory benefit system has changed.

Why is this opening sentence better?

This is a better opening sentence because it states a point of view and provides a platform for several examples on both sides of the argument to be introduced, discussed and linked back to the question. It does not give a conclusion too early. It gives scope for evidence and discussion in the paragraph to lead to the mini-conclusion of how much the founding principle has changed. Think of your first statement as an opinion which you have to justify and assess in the rest of the paragraph.

Step 3

Choose an example that can be explained.

This is a weak example.

 For example, Pension Credit is not available to all pensioners only those that have an income below £109 per week. This is not in line with the founding principle.

Why is this example weak?

This example is weak because it is too specific and factual. It makes further development almost impossible. Your example should be one which can be explained and expanded with further examples and mini-points. Try to avoid examples which are simply a list of facts. Your example should open up discussion, not close it down.

This is a better example.

 For example, the government's policy of 'progressive universalism' means that an increasing number of government benefits are means tested or 'targeted' and therefore not available to everyone.

Why is this example better?

This example is better because it allows for further more specific examples of benefits to be given to back it up. It sets up the line of argument to be discussed and judged in the paragraph. This example opens up the paragraph and allows other relevant points to be brought in.

Step 4

Explain and expand your example. This is where you make your line of argument clear and develop it by providing evidence to support the point you are making.

 Explain In the past, benefits were universal; they were available to everyone. People contributed through National Insurance and received a flat-rate benefit set at a level that kept them out of poverty. However, now there is more means testing and much tougher rules about claiming. **Expand** In the case of the elderly, the basic state pension is no longer sufficient to meet the needs of many pensioners. The government tackled this problem not by increasing the flat-rate but by targeting the neediest through a means-tested Pension Credit. Single pensioners with an income below £119·05 and couples with an income below £181·70 can apply for a pension credit to make up the difference and raise their income.

You could further develop this paragraph by discussing other benefits like Income Support, Job Seeker's Allowance and proposed changes to Incapacity Benefit. If you want to provide balance within your paragraph you could argue that tax credits are still close to founding principles because they are available to all but the very rich.

Step 5

Link your paragraph. This is where you provide balanced comment and explain how the information in the paragraph relates to what the question asks. **1** Is it for or against? Is it a good point or a bad point? Does it show a strong point or a weakness in the argument? It is also a good idea to link your paragraph to the next section of your essay. **2** This allows your argument to flow.

 It can therefore be argued that very few current benefits are in line with the founding principle of universalism. Most have an element of targeting and means testing not present when the welfare state was set up. **1** The erosion of the universal principle does not only apply to the benefit system. **2**

Here is another example of a paragraph developed with PEA.

EXAM EXAMPLE 3

> **Critically examine the effectiveness of Congress and the Supreme Court in limiting the powers of the President.**
>
> *Study Theme 3C: The United States of America*

This is a very good paragraph.

P Under the American Constitution the powers of the three branches of the government are separated so that, as one of the founding fathers, Thomas Jefferson said, 'no one could transcend their legal limits without being effectively checked and restrained by the others.' This means that, constitutionally, the power of the President can be limited by Congress and the Supreme Court. **E** For example, this is particularly apparent when it comes to raising taxes to pay for Presidential programmes. **A – explain** The President decides his priorities and prepares a budget which he sends to Congress. However, the President cannot pay for his programmes until Congress has approved them and passed a law authorising him to raise taxes. **A – expand** The President often faces opposition to his plans, particularly when the majority in Congress are from a different party. For example, Republican President Bush submitted his 2008 budget to Congress with plans to reduce spending on social programmes like Medicare and Medicaid and to increase spending on defence, including proposals for a missile intercept system in Europe. However, the Democratic Congress refused to vote funding for the missile programme. **A – link** In this way, Congress was effective in limiting the power of President Bush by denying him the money to carry out one of his policies. **1** This is not the only way in which the power of the President can be limited. **2**

Why is this a very good paragraph?

This is a very good paragraph because it is fully developed and flowing. The first point **P** is made in a way that allows the paragraph to grow. The example **E** chosen is one that can be analysed in depth. The explanation **A – explain** connects back to the example and forward to the next part of the paragraph. This means that the paragraph can be smoothly expanded **A – expand** with an associated idea and further example to advance the argument. At the end of the paragraph **A – link** there are two types of links – a mini-conclusion linking back to the question **1** and a link forward to the next part of the essay. **2**

> These examples may not be from one of your study themes, but the PEA technique can be used for all study themes. Try building a paragraph using PEA to answer a question from one of your study themes. You can use one of the examples of exam questions from earlier in the chapter.

Balance

Modern Studies essays must have **balance** – you must **always** give arguments on both sides **and** comment on the issue.

How do I show balance?

You can do this within a paragraph or as a separate section of your essay. Generally, it is easier to answer *'to what extent'*, *'assess'* and *'discuss'* by giving both sides of the argument in each paragraph and for *'examine'* or *'critically examine'* questions it is often easier to provide the counter argument in a separate section.

In the end, the style you use depends on how you prefer to write your answers and what you feel most comfortable with.

EXAM EXAMPLE 1

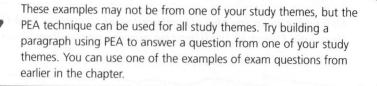

> **There are fairer electoral systems than First Past the Post. Discuss.**
>
> *Study Theme 1D: Electoral Systems, Voting and Political Attitudes*

Here is a very good example of balance within a paragraph.

P One of the claims made for Proportional Representation (PR) systems, like the Additional Member System (AMS) used for elections to the

Scottish Parliament, is that they are fairer than First Past the Post because they more truly reflect the wishes of the electorate. **E** For example, with the First Past the Post system smaller parties are under-represented because they receive more votes than seats, whereas the opposite is true for larger parties. This imbalance was amply demonstrated in the 2005 General Election where the Liberal Democrats won over one-fifth of the votes (22%) but less than one-tenth (9·6%) of the seats in the House of Commons. In comparison, the over-representation of the Labour Party, who received just over one-third (35%) of the votes and over half (55%) of the seats, was apparent. **A – explain** This shows that the simple majority, 'winner takes all' rule of the First Past the Post system, which resulted in Labour forming a majority government despite only 21% of the total electorate voting for them, has an inbuilt unfairness. **A – expand** Furthermore, this is in sharp contrast to the AMS used for the 2007 elections for the Scottish Parliament. In this case, the imbalance in the First Past the Post constituency vote, where the Scottish National Party (SNP) won more votes but fewer seats than Labour, was corrected by the proportional representation regional list vote with the SNP eventually winning 32% of the votes and 35% of the seats. **A – link** A much fairer result because, unlike the outcome with First Past the Post, it truly reflected the wishes of the voters as demonstrated at the ballot box. **Balance** **BP** On the other hand, it is possible to argue that the First Past the Post system also reflects the wishes of the electorate because when people are voting they are expressing their desire for the government of their choice. **BE** For example, under First Past the Post Labour obtained a majority of 66 seats in the 2005 General Election. **BA – explain** This means that, unlike the SNP in Scotland, Labour can govern without the support of other parties and implement their manifesto promises. Labour received more votes than any other party and this is precisely what the people who voted for them wished for – a strong government capable of carrying out the policies their supporters wanted and reacting decisively to events. **BA – expand** In comparison, the AMS in Scotland resulted in a minority SNP Scottish Government that will have to take account of the views of other parties in order to govern effectively. It can be argued that this does not truly reflect the wishes of the people who voted for the SNP in the belief that they would be able to carry out their manifesto promises. **BA – link** However, overall the question of whether an electoral system is 'fair' depends on what you wish it to achieve. If the aim is to reflect the voters' wish for a government with a working majority, able to carry out its election pledges, then First Past the Post is 'fair' because it usually achieves that. Alternatively, if the wish of the electorate is for seats to reflect the number of votes and for there to be a minority government or a power sharing coalition, then PR systems are 'fairer' because that is the usual outcome.

Why is this a very good example of balance within a paragraph?

This is a very good example because the change of direction is clearly shown. Balance The opposite point of view BP connects back to the first part of the paragraph. The example BE also connects with previous evidence and is one that can be analysed. The explanation BA – explain connects back to the example and the first part of the paragraph. The balance is expanded BA – expand with a further example and opinion. At the end of the paragraph BA – link there is balanced comment in a mini-conclusion giving an opinion on the evidence in the paragraph and linking it back to the issue in the question.

> The 'link' part of your paragraph is where you provide balanced comment by giving an opinion about how the information in the paragraph relates to the issue in the question. Look back at the section on effective writing in Chapter 1 to remind yourself of words and phrases that you can use to show emphasis.

Here is a very good example of a separate paragraph showing the other side of the argument.

EXAM EXAMPLE 2

> **Critically examine the effectiveness of Congress and the Supreme Court in limiting the powers of the President.**
>
> *Study Theme 3C: The United States of America*

BP On the other hand, despite the limits that the Constitution allows Congress and the Supreme Court to impose on the President, the Presidency has significant powers of its own which can be used to effectively 'check' the other two branches of the American government. BE For example, the President can veto (refuse to sign) Congressional legislation as President Bush did in 2006 with a bill on stem cell research. BA – explain Even though Congress can override a Presidential veto with a two-thirds majority in both the House of Representatives and the Senate, it is not a very realistic check because it is extremely difficult to achieve such a majority. In fact, it is more common for the threat of a Presidential veto to force Congress to amend legislation in the President's favour as happened in 2004 when President Bush threatened to veto the Liability Bill on gun control because it contained a Democratic amendment to include a ban on assault weapons. BA – expand Furthermore, it is common for the President to by-pass Congress by issuing Executive Orders. President Bush has issued 245 of these so far in his two terms of office. These included two that extended Presidential powers in the wake of the 9/11 terrorist attack. The Homeland Security Department was set up by Executive Order and only later confirmed by Act of Congress. Similarly, President Bush issued an Executive Order giving the Attorney General power to overrule the courts if they ordered the release of a terrorist. Congress later confirmed this with the Patriot Act. BA – link The fact that Congress approved this significant extension of Presidential power with little or no opposition shows that Congress finds it difficult to limit the actions of a popular President, especially in a time of national emergency. 1 In addition, the President has a number of powers that he can use to counteract 'checks' by the Supreme Court. 2

Why is this a very good example of a separate paragraph showing balance?

The change of direction is clearly shown by the wording and the start of a new paragraph. The first point BP refers to the previous section of the essay and connects back to the question. The example given BE is one that can be analysed in depth. The explanation BA – explain connects back to the example and the first section of the essay. The balance is expanded BA – expand with further examples and comment. A line of argument is developed by linking back to the previous section and rebutting (arguing against) the points made. At the end of the paragraph BA – link there is a mini-conclusion that sums up and links back to the question. 1 There is also a link forward to the next paragraph. 2

The 'expand' part of your paragraph is where you develop your line of argument by linking back and moving forward. Link back to earlier sections of the essay, support or rebut previous points and then move forward by adding more information to support your point of view. Look back at the section on effective writing in Chapter 1 to remind yourself of words and phrases that will help you do this.

Length

You have **20 minutes** to write your essay in the exam, so length will also depend on how much you can write in that time.

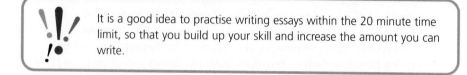

It is a good idea to practise writing essays within the 20 minute time limit, so that you build up your skill and increase the amount you can write.

How much should I write for my middle section?

If you are providing balance within your paragraph you should aim for at least three fully developed paragraphs. You can use this structure as a guideline.

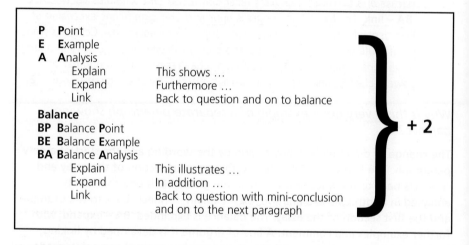

P   **P**oint
E   **E**xample
A   **A**nalysis
     Explain   This shows …
     Expand   Furthermore …
     Link   Back to question and on to balance

Balance
BP **B**alance **P**oint
BE **B**alance **E**xample
BA **B**alance **A**nalysis
     Explain   This illustrates …
     Expand   In addition …
     Link   Back to question with mini-conclusion
                and on to the next paragraph

} + 2

If you are providing balance in a separate section you should aim for at least three developed paragraphs supporting your decision and at least two against. You could use a structure like this.

P Point
E Example
A Analysis
     Explain   This shows …
     Expand   Furthermore …
     Link   Back to question with mini-conclusion
                      and on to the next section
	+ 2

Balance Section
P Point
E Example
A Analysis
     Explain   This illustrates …
     Expand   In addition …
     Link   Back to question with mini-conclusion
                      and on to the next section
	+ 1

These are guidelines and suggestions to give you a structure to build on. There is no single 'recipe' for writing the middle section of an essay, but the basic 'ingredients' are the ones shown above. Markers are looking for individual style and flair. It is a good idea, once you have a basic structure, to try putting the 'ingredients' together in your own way. If you practise this, your confidence will grow and your own writing style will emerge.

WRITING A CONCLUSION

A conclusion at the end is a sign of a mature candidate, as long as it is a conclusion and not a summary of previous points. Integrated conclusions are perfectly acceptable when signalled by appropriate words and phrases.

Principal Assessor's Report

The markers will accept an essay without a conclusion, as long as you provided balanced comment by drawing mini-conclusions throughout your essay. However, writing a short conclusion is a good way to pull the various points of your argument together.

In your conclusion you must make your mind up about the issue raised in the question and:

❶ state your decision or judgement

❷ prioritise your main points.

Do not make rash statements in your conclusion, no matter how strongly you feel about an issue. Your conclusion must be balanced. Do not introduce new facts. Your conclusion must be based on the information in your essay. Make a balanced comment by reconsidering what you have written and decide which of the points you raised in your introduction and analysed in your essay are the most important in answering the question.

EXAM EXAMPLE 1

> ***There are fairer electoral systems than First Past the Post. Discuss.***
>
> *Study Theme 1D: Electoral Systems, Voting and Political Attitudes*

This conclusion is weak.

Therefore, there are fairer systems than First Past the Post. Proportional representation systems like the Additional Member System are fairer because they have a closer link between votes and seats, voters have more choice, smaller parties get more seats, votes are not wasted and there is more consensus-style government because the winning party needs the co-operation of other parties to get things done.

Why is this conclusion weak?

This conclusion is weak because it does not make the judgement the question asks for. If the writer believes proportional representation systems are fairer, the conclusion must state how much fairer by making some reference to the other side of the discussion. This is a summary rather than a conclusion. The main points in the essay are simply listed with no attempt to prioritise and judge which are the most important.

Here is a much better conclusion.

Therefore, the question of whether there are fairer systems than First Past the Post depends on what is meant by 'fair'. **1** If 'fair' means a close link between the votes cast and seats gained, smaller parties having greater representation and consensus-style coalition government then proportional representation systems are 'fairer'. In Scotland, a power-sharing, multi-party Scottish Parliament was the aim and the Additional Member System was thought to be 'fairer' because it would achieve this. However, if the measure of 'fairness' is a close link between elected members and their constituencies and a majority government with no need to compromise its policies because it is not under the influence of smaller parties then First Past the Post is 'fair' and achieves this for the House of Commons. **2** In the end, the 'fairness' of an electoral system depends on what outcome is required.

Why is this conclusion much better?

This conclusion is much better because it makes the judgement the question asks for. **1** The writer provides a balanced comment that the question of fairness is open to interpretation and the marker can see that the candidate has fully understood the requirements of a 'discuss' question. The writer justifies their opinion by prioritising reasons on both sides of the argument. **2** This is more than a summary because it highlights the main line of argument in the essay and brings it to a close in a persuasive and convincing manner. The marker can see that the writer has fully understood the issue in the question.

Here is another example of how to write a conclusion.

EXAM EXAMPLE 2

> **To what extent are the founding principles of the welfare state being met?**
>
> *Study Theme 2: Wealth and Health Inequalities in the United Kingdom*

Therefore, although the state still provides services from the 'cradle to the grave', the welfare state's founding principles of universal, collective and comprehensive are not being entirely met. **1** Most benefits are now targeted and means-tested and this undermines the principle of universal, contributory, flat-rate benefits. The collectivist and comprehensive principles of the state providing equal services do not entirely apply now that Private-Public Partnerships build many hospitals and schools, housing associations rather than local councils provide rented housing and dentists and opticians charge for services. 2

This is a very good conclusion because it links immediately to the question and gives a well-balanced decision 1 based on the information in the question. It prioritises the reasons for the decision in a persuasive manner 2 so the marker can see the writer has fully understood the question and provided a convincing argument to answer it.

Here is another reminder of how to write a good conclusion.

EXAM EXAMPLE 3

> **Critically examine the effectiveness of Congress and the Supreme Court in limiting the powers of the President.**
>
> *Study Theme 3C: The United States of America*

Therefore Congress and the Supreme Court are only effective in limiting the powers of the President to a certain extent because it depends on their ability and willingness to do so. 1 A strong, popular President can use constitutional powers, patronage and electoral strength to control Congress, whereas a 'lame duck' President at the end of his term of office will find this difficult. The Supreme Court can declare the President's actions unconstitutional and Congress can impeach him, but the status of the Office of President means that these powers are rarely used. 2

Your conclusion should give a definite statement that makes your decision completely clear. It should also reiterate your line of argument and clearly point out the balance of evidence that lead you to your decision. In the previous examples from this question, the writer argued that the limiting powers of Congress and the Supreme Court are only effective against the President in certain circumstances. This decision is now confidently stated in the conclusion. 1 The writer then restates the line of argument that the powers and status of the President are such that Congress and Supreme Court can rarely limit them and highlights the main evidence in the essay that backs up this argument. 2

You can apply this technique to all of your conclusions.

MARKING ESSAYS

Pass or better answers must feature both knowledge and understanding of the issue and analysis of/balanced comment on the issue.

Higher Modern Studies Marking Instructions

What advice does the SQA give?

The SQA says:

> *Candidates should integrate knowledge and understanding and analysis and communicate these effectively in a coherent, logically structured way. Arguments should be supported by up-to-date evidence and analysis should be balanced and informed showing a high level of awareness of political and social issues.*

You can 'translate' this into what markers are looking for.

Markers like ...		Markers dislike ...	
Strong start	✔	'Turning' the question	✘
Focus on the question	✔	Too little information	✘
Strong line of argument	✔	Simplistic references	✘
Analysis and discussion	✔	Failure to develop points	✘
Recent examples	✔	Out of date examples	✘
Links back to the question	✔	No linkage to question	✘
Balanced comment	✔	Lack of balance	✘
Links between sections	✔	Lists and bullet points	✘
Conclusion that prioritises	✔	Summary instead of conclusion	✘

Does the SQA give advice about what makes a Grade A essay?

Yes. The SQA says that a Grade A essay should:

- Demonstrate knowledge and understanding by:
  - providing accurate and extended descriptions of issues
  - making reference to relevant
    complex factors,
    institutions,
    and detailed examples

- Demonstrate skills of analysis
  - in well-balanced way
  - with relevant and detailed exemplification
  - by reaching relevant well-developed conclusions

Can I get a list of what to include in an essay for a good pass?

Yes. The following essay marking grid shows you what achieves good marks in an essay. Markers read through your essay to decide if it is a pass before reading it again to give it a mark. Make sure your information, accuracy and writing style will impress the marker on first reading.

Markers use only whole marks so you must make sure you fully explain, expand and link your information. The marks for each grade are:

C	8
B	9–10
A	11–15

Use the grid to mark your own essays. It is a good idea if you are not doing well in an area of essay writing to look back at that section of this chapter and see how you can move up the grid from pass, to good pass to very good pass.

ESSAY MARKING GRID

Pass		Good Pass		Very Good Pass	

Introduction

Links to the question		Clear link to the quesiton		Convincing link to the question	
Makes a decision		Makes a considered decision		Makes a carefully planned decision	
Sets out how the question will be answered		Clearly sets out both sides of argument		Persuasively sets out both sides of argument	

Main Body

Knowledge and Understanding

Enough information to answer the question		Detailed information linked to question		Extensive information directly linked to question	
Accurate descriptions		Accurate and detailed descriptions		Accurate and extended descriptions	
Suitable, up-to-date examples		Relevant, up-to-date examples		Detailed, current, insightful examples	

Analysis

Explanation of why information used		Relevant explanation of why information used		Detailed explanation of why information used	
Discussion of issue raised in the question		Detailed discussion of issue raised in question		Expansive discussion of issue raised in the question	
Different point of view discussed		Well argued points of view		Detailed well argued points of view	

Conclusion

| Decision based on information given | | Balanced decision based on information | | Well-balanced decision based on information | |
| Summarises reasons for decision | | Prioritises reasons for decisions | | Persuasively prioritises reasons for decision | |

Essay Style

Proper structure of sentences/paragraphs		Developed, linked paragraphs		Fully developed, flowing paragraphs	
Few errors in spelling or punctuation		Correct spelling/ punctuation		No errors in spelling or punctuation	
Expresses ideas confidently		Expresses ideas convincingly		Fluent, flowing style, persuasively linking ideas	

Glossary

Analysis – Detailed assessment

Appropriate – Relevant

Argument – A line of thought

Assess – To weigh up how much

Balance – A presentation of both sides of an argument

Balanced comment – Giving an opinion about both sides of an issue

Balanced conclusion – A conclusion which considers both sides of an argument

Criteria – Standards by which something is judged

Critically examine – To judge how good

Description – Statement of the features of a particular issue

Discuss – To consider how accurate

Examine – How good

Example – Evidence

Expand – Provide information to make an argument more convincing

Explain – Give more detail to make main points clearer

Explicit – Clear and exact

Factor – Reason or event

Flair – Distinctive, confident style

Flaw – Fault or weakness

Fluent and flowing – Effortless writing style linking ideas

Fully developed paragraph – A paragraph that contains all the elements of PEA

Illustrate – Provide examples, make comparisons

Introduction – Opening paragraph that sets out the course of the essay

Issue – A topic of discussion

Knowledge and understanding – Information learned

Line of argument – Key opinion that runs through the whole essay

Link – Connecting sentence

Mini-conclusion – A conclusion at the end of each PEA

Point of view – Opinion

Prioritise – Rank

Rebut – Provide a solution to arguments against your point of view

Relevant – Appropriate and applicable

Specific – Exact

Study theme – Area of study

Style – Manner of writing

Synthesis – Combining ideas and information

Technique – Skill

To what extent – To assess how much

Topic sentence – Sentence that sets out the point of view of the paragraph

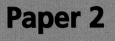

3   Paper 2

INTRODUCTION TO PAPER 2

This is a skills-based paper which enables well trained candidates to achieve high marks.

Principal Assessor's Report

Paper 2 contains the sources and questions for your Decision Making Exercise.

What skills will I need for my Decision Making Exercise?

To get a good grade for your Decision Making Exercise you have to read for information and handle data from sources. You have to evaluate this information to answer questions. But, more importantly, you have to put it together (synthesise it) with background information to write a report.

Look at Chapter 1 if you need to brush up on any of these skills!

What topic does my Decision Making Exercise cover?

Your Decision Making Exercise (DME) is based on unit 2 – Social Issues in the United Kingdom. The topic is *Wealth and Health Inequalities in the UK*.

What do I have to do?

There will be only **one** Decision Making Exercise. It will be in **two** parts:

❶ **Evaluating questions** based only on the sources in the paper – worth 10 marks.

❷ **Decision making task** in which you adopt a role, prepare and write a report – worth 20 marks.

The front page of the paper will have instructions like this:

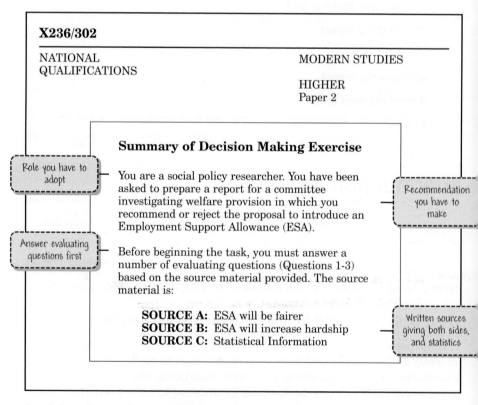

X236/302

NATIONAL
QUALIFICATIONS

MODERN STUDIES

HIGHER
Paper 2

Summary of Decision Making Exercise

Role you have to adopt

You are a social policy researcher. You have been asked to prepare a report for a committee investigating welfare provision in which you recommend or reject the proposal to introduce an Employment Support Allowance (ESA).

Recommendation you have to make

Answer evaluating questions first

Before beginning the task, you must answer a number of evaluating questions (Questions 1-3) based on the source material provided. The source material is:

SOURCE A: ESA will be fairer
SOURCE B: ESA will increase hardship
SOURCE C: Statistical Information

Written sources giving both sides, and statistics

Read these instructions carefully because you need to have your role, the decision you have to make and what the statistics show clear in your mind before you start answering the questions.

TIMING

Candidates should be aware of the importance of time management.

Principal Assessor's Report

Getting your timing right is vital to achieving a good grade in Paper 2. You have to plan ahead and use the time you are given to your best advantage.

How much time do I have to complete Paper 2?

You have 1 hour 15 minutes (75 minutes) to complete the evaluating questions and prepare and write your report.

How many marks is Paper 2 worth?

Paper 2 is worth 30 marks – the evaluating questions are worth 10 marks and your report is worth 20 marks

How should I divide my time?

You have 75 minutes to complete the paper. Try and divide your time like this:

10 minutes	– read instructions and sources
15–20 minutes	– answer evaluating questions
40 minutes	– write report
5 minutes	– check over report and questions

Should I skip planning my report?

No. The main reason for getting a poor grade in Paper 2 is not planning your report. You must combine all the sources and your background knowledge under appropriate headings to justify your recommendation. You cannot do this unless you give yourself time to make notes and plan what you are going to write.

THE EVALUATING QUESTIONS

Candidates should always answer the evaluating questions before doing the task.

Principal Assessor's Report

Why do I have to answer the evaluating questions first?

You must answer the evaluating questions first because it gives you an opportunity to read through each source before you attempt your report. There are three main sources – written sources A and B giving opposing views and Source C giving statistical information. The evaluating questions combine written and statistical sources and direct you to the main argument and points you need for your report. They also give you clues about what background knowledge to include.

How long should I spend on evaluating questions?

Spend no more than 20 minutes on evaluating questions. Keep your answers short and use only the sources you are directed to.

How do I answer evaluating questions?

To answer the evaluating questions, bring together information from different sources and come to a conclusion. Do not bring in background information: use only the information in the sources.

What kinds of evaluating questions will I be asked?

Evaluating questions are based only on the source material in the exam paper. These sources might be newspaper articles, viewpoints and statistical tables, graphs and maps. You will be told which sources to use and asked to:

- detect and explain – bias, exaggeration, selective use of facts
- decide if the evidence supports a view
- compare or contrast views

What is a 'detect and explain' question?

You will usually get at least one question that asks you to judge exaggeration or selective use of the facts. Here are some past questions.

Example 1

> *Use only Source C1 and Source B.*
>
> **Quote an example of exaggeration by Erica Tate. Give a reason for your choice.** (2)
>
> *2003 Decision Making Exercise 1*

Example 2

> *Use only Source C3 and Source A.*
>
> **Why might David McQueen be accused of exaggeration?** (2)
>
> *2006 Decision Making Exercise 1*

Example 3

> *Use only Source C1 and Source A.*
>
> **In what way is the Inverbromie Clarion selective in the use of facts? Give evidence to support your choice.** (2)
>
> *2003 Decision Making Exercise 2*

How do I answer 'detect and explain' questions?

Write out exemplars of exaggeration and selectivity in full.

Principal Assessor's Report

All these questions ask you to detect and explain exaggeration or selectivity. They direct you to the sources and tell you not to use any other sources or background information. Each question is worth two marks. To answer a question like this you do two things, one from each source:

❶ Detect and quote an example of exaggeration or selectivity from the written source.

❷ Use evidence from the statistical source to explain why it is exaggerated or selective.

How do I find the example I need?

The quickest way is to look at the statistical source first to see what it is about. This tells you what you are looking for in the written statement. The exam example below will help you with this.

EXAM EXAMPLE 1

> *Use only Source C1 and Source B.*
>
> **Quote an example of exaggeration by Erica Tate. Give a reason for your choice.**   **(2)**
>
> *2003 Decision Making Exercise 1*

SOURCE B: "POSITIVE ACTION IS UNNECESSARY" (Extract)

... Almost 7% of our population now comes from an ethnic minority background. For London the figure is estimated to reach 40% by 2004. Most of our large cities are now a vibrant mix of cultures and identities. Employers select on the basis of skills – not skin. Racial differences in unemployment are almost non-existent. The present generation of ethnic minorities is willing and able to take advantage of the many opportunities available in the UK ...

Erica Tate, Labour Party Activist

SOURCE C1:   Unemployment in the UK – selected ethnic groups by area

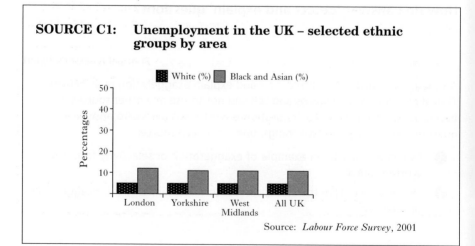

Source: *Labour Force Survey*, 2001

Using DATA (see Chapter 1) you can quickly see that the statistical source shows Blacks and Asians have higher unemployment than Whites. This tells you that the exaggerated statement is something to do with unemployment and race and if it is exaggerated it probably is the opposite of what the statistics show. You can now quickly scan the written source looking for an incorrect statement about race and employment.

Here is a weak answer to the question.

'Racial differences ... non-existent' is exaggerated because Blacks and Asians have higher unemployment.

Why is this answer weak?

This answer is weak because the statement is not written out in full. The sources are not named and there are no figures from the sources to prove exaggeration.

Here is a better answer to the question.

In Source B, Erica Tate says: 'Racial differences in unemployment are almost non-existent.' This is exaggerated because Source C1 shows that throughout the UK percentage unemployment for Blacks and Asians is double that of Whites – a UK average of 10% for Blacks and Asians, compared with 5% for Whites.

Why is this answer better?

The source is named and the statement is quoted in full. Do not be tempted to abbreviate: examiners do not like it – always write the statement in full. The answer fully explains the exaggeration using figures from the statistical source.

Speed and accuracy are important in this part of the paper, so remember the steps to finding and writing your answer quickly.

1. Read the question.
2. Look at the statistical source first – work out what you are looking for.
3. Read the written source – find the statement you need.
4. Quote the statement in full.
5. Quote evidence from the statistical source to prove exaggeration or selectivity.

EXAM EXAMPLE 2

> ### Use only Source C2 and Source A.
>
> ### Why might Charlie Dunne be accused of exaggeration?   (2)
>
> *2005 Decision Making Exercise 2*

SOURCE A: FOUNDING A NEW APPROACH TO HEALTH CARE (Extract)

In recent years, there have been record increases in health spending. The NHS is now one of the fastest growing health systems in Europe. Not only does the public have complete trust in the Government's ability to improve the NHS but there is no longer any opposition to private sector involvement in the NHS. However, investment must be matched by reform if the large sums of money now going into the NHS are to be spent effectively …

Charlie Dunne, Medical Practice Manager

SOURCE C2:   Public Opinion Survey

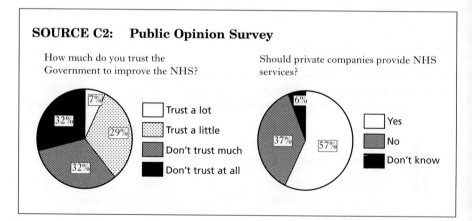

How much do you trust the Government to improve the NHS?

- 7% Trust a lot
- 29% Trust a little
- 32% Don't trust much
- 32% Don't trust at all

Should private companies provide NHS services?

- 57% Yes
- 37% No
- 6% Don't know

Look at the statistical source first. This source is analysed in Chapter 1, so you can turn back to remind yourself how to do this if you need to. The source is about trust in the government to improve the NHS and support for private companies providing NHS services. This tells you to look for something Charlie Dunne says about this and then check the survey to see in what way it is exaggerated.

Here is a weak answer to the question.

In Source A, the statement 'Not only ... the NHS' is exaggerated because Source C2 shows 32% don't trust at all and 29% don't trust much.

Why is this answer weak?

This answer is weak because the statement is not written out in full and some of the information in the source has been missed out. Information has simply been copied from the source with little attempt to analyse it.

Here is a better answer.

Charlie Dunne's claim in Source A that: 'Not only does the public have complete trust in the government's ability to improve the NHS but there is no longer any opposition to private sector involvement in the NHS' is exaggerated. It is exaggerated because Source C2 shows that over 50% of those surveyed do not trust the government much or at all. When asked if private companies should provide NHS services, 37% of those surveyed said 'no', which shows there is still some opposition to private sector involvement.

Why is this answer better?

This is answer is better because the exaggerated statement is quoted in full. Information is given from the two pie charts. It has been analysed and recalculated to be to the best advantage in proving exaggeration.

How do I answer a 'to what extent' question?

A significant number of candidates omitted the balance necessary in their responses to achieve full marks in the 'to what extent' evaluating questions.

Principal Assessor's Report

'To what extent' questions require a balanced answer. Here is an example of a question.

EXAM EXAMPLE

> *Use only Source C2 and Source B2.*
>
> **To what extent is Georgina Burns selective in the use of facts?** **(3)**
>
> *2002 Decision Making Exercise 2*

SOURCE B2: MEANS TESTING MEANS BETTER VALUE FOR MONEY!

The numbers of old people in all elderly age groups are set to rise for the foreseeable future. As people grow older they develop more health problems and need more care. This means that the cost of providing free personal care will take up a huge percentage of the UK's wealth. It is much more sensible to continue to means test care. Those who can afford to contribute should do so. In Scotland most old people do not have to pay for their care at present. Only 7000 relatively well off Scottish pensioners are likely to benefit from making personal care free for all. The elderly are more affected by poverty than other groups in UK society but they already receive more public money in the form of benefits than any other group. There are more urgent priorities for government spending than paying for the care of those elderly people who have decent pensions and valuable property.

Georgina Burns

SOURCE C2:   Benefits and income for certain groups in the UK

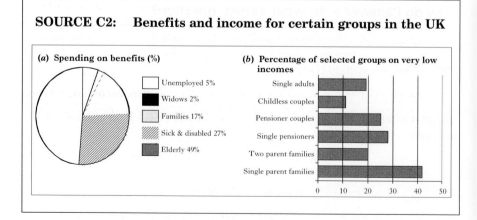

(a) **Spending on benefits (%)**

- ☐ Unemployed 5%
- ■ Widows 2%
- ☐ Families 17%
- ▨ Sick & disabled 27%
- ▩ Elderly 49%

(b) **Percentage of selected groups on very low incomes**

Single adults
Childless couples
Pensioner couples
Single pensioners
Two parent families
Single parent families

0   10   20   30   40   50

The question asks you to make a judgement about how selective Georgina Burns is. You must show balance by giving evidence for and against her being selective.

The question is worth 3 marks and you have to do three things:

❶ Detect a passage from the written source that shows selectivity.

❷ Find statistical evidence to explain what part of the statement is correct.

❸ Find statistical evidence to explain what part of the statement is wrong.

Here is a weak answer to the question.

The elderly are more affected by poverty than other groups in UK society but they already receive more public money in the form of benefits than any other group.

Why is this answer weak?

This answer is weak because although there is an attempt at balance, there is no evidence from the sources to prove that it is correct.

Here is a better answer.

In Source B2, Georgina claims that the elderly 'receive more public money in the form of benefits than any other group'. This statement is correct because Source C2(a) shows that, at 49%, the elderly are the group with the highest amount of spending on benefits. However, Georgina also claims that the 'elderly are more affected by poverty than other groups in UK society'. Georgina has been selective because Source C2(b) shows this to be incorrect – single parent families are the group with the lowest incomes.

Why is this answer better?

This answer is better because it is balanced and gives evidence from the sources. It quotes the part of Georgina's statement that is correct and proves this with evidence from the statistical source. It also quotes the part of the statement that is incorrect and clearly points out the evidence in the statistical source which proves Georgina has been selective in the use of facts.

What is a 'supporting a view' question?

You will usually get at least one question that asks you to find evidence to support a view. Here are some past questions.

Example 1

> *Use only Source C1 and Source B2.*
>
> **What evidence is there to support the view of Ailsa Hamilton?** (2)
>
> *Question 2(a) 2002 Decision Making Exercise 1*

This is a 2 mark question which involves you quoting the statement from the written source and quoting the evidence from the statistical source which supports it.

Example 2

> *Use only Source C3 and Source B2.*
>
> **What evidence is there both for and against the view of Tricia Williams?** (3)
>
> *2000 Decision Making Exercise 1*

This is a 3 mark question where you have to quote the view from the written source and then find evidence from the statistical source which supports the view and evidence which does not support it.

How do I answer a 'supporting a view' question?

There is an unwelcome tendency for candidates to feature the 'first …………last' words of 'views': this is not acceptable; quotes or sentences should be written out in full.

Principal Assessor's Report

The most common type of 'supporting a view' question is a 'to what extent' one. Here is an example of a question.

EXAM EXAMPLE

> **Use only Source C1 and Source A.**
>
> **To what extent does the evidence support Russell Barclay?**   (3)
>
> *2007 Decision Making Exercise*

SOURCE A: ESA WILL BE FAIRER (Extract)

... In Scotland, over 300,000 people receive Incapacity Benefit. In Glasgow, one in five of those of working age claim this benefit. Incapacity Benefit increases after six months and again after a year. It is paid for life and may be accompanied by other benefits. Incapacity Benefit discourages people from seeking work. No wonder long-term sickness and disability is the most common reason given for both men and women for not working. It is not just older workers who qualify for Incapacity Benefit – each month over a thousand teenagers claim it. We are encouraging welfare dependency at the expense of individual responsibility. Incapacity Benefit needs reform ...

SOURCE C1:   Reasons given by people of working age for not working

Male	Reasons	Female
%		%
37	Long-term sickness/disability	21
6	Looking after family/home	45
30	Student	19
13	Early retirement	4
14	Other	11

Source: Adapted from Labour Force Survey, Office for National Statistics

This 'to what extent' question is worth 3 marks, so you have to do three things:

1 Detect a passage from the written source that gives Russell Barclay's view.

2 Find statistical evidence that supports the view.

3 Find statistical evidence that disagrees with the view.

Look at the statistical source first to find out what you are looking for. The table is about reasons given by males and females for not working, so you are looking for Russell Barclay's view as to why men and women do not work.

Here is a weak answer to the question.

The evidence supports Russell Barclay a bit because men do not work because of sickness and disability but for women it is looking after the home and family.

Why is this answer weak?

This answer is weak because although there is an attempt at balance, it does not give the view or use figures from the statistical source to back up what it says.

Here is a better answer.

Russell Barclay's view in Source A that 'long-term sickness and disability is the most common reason given for both men and women for not working' is only partly supported by the evidence. Source C1 shows that, at 37%, long-term sickness and disability is the most common reason given by men for not working. However, this is not the case for women – at 45%, looking after family and home is the most common reason given by women for not working.

Why is this answer better?

This answer is better because it is balanced. It quotes the view and immediately explains it is only supported to a certain extent. It then gives evidence that shows support for the view and contrasts this with evidence that disproves the view.

What is a 'compare and contrast' question?

You might be asked to compare or contrast the views in the written sources. These questions are useful for seeing the two sides of the issue on which you have to make a recommendation. Here are some past questions:

Example 1

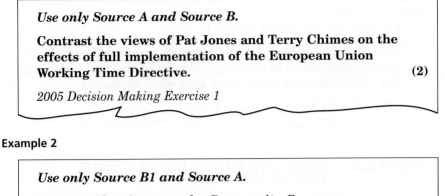

> *Use only Source A and Source B.*
>
> **Contrast the views of Pat Jones and Terry Chimes on the effects of full implementation of the European Union Working Time Directive.** **(2)**
>
> *2005 Decision Making Exercise 1*

Example 2

> *Use only Source B1 and Source A.*
>
> **Contrast the views on why Community Care was introduced.** **(2)**
>
> *2002 Decision Making Exercise 2*

Example 3

> *Use only Source A and Source B.*
>
> **In what way do Ashley Frasier and Erica Tate differ in their view of Labour's record on tackling racism?** **(2)**
>
> *2003 Decision Making Exercise 1*

How do I answer a 'compare and contrast' question?

Some candidates are failing to give both viewpoints in 'contrast' questions.

Principal Assessor's Report

The question directs you to the view you have to compare. Read the question carefully and make sure you are only comparing views on the topic in the question. Read through the written sources and quote the different views on this topic. Here is an example of a question.

EXAM EXAMPLE

> **Use only Source A and Source B.**
>
> **Contrast the views of David McQueen and Lisa Newman on the circumstances in which people would end their working days if compulsory retirement ages were abolished.** **(2)**
>
> *2006 Decision Making Exercise 1*

SOURCE A: FACING UP TO THE DEMOGRAPHIC TIME BOMB (Extract)

... Scrapping retirement age does not mean that people should remain in paid employment regardless of fitness or competence. Employers already use trade union approved methods to monitor and evaluate the performance of staff. However, it would mean a change to the circumstances in which long service employees ended their working days. Instead of being "pensioned off", they could now retire with dignity. With government placing such a large emphasis on the importance of giving choice in other areas of social policy, it is surely time to extend it to employment ...

SOURCE B: KEEP COMPULSORY RETIREMENT AGES (Extract)

... Admittedly, some may be financially unprepared for retirement, but this has less to do with demography and more to do with gaps in their employment record. Whereas the efforts of social inclusion policies to keep such gaps to a minimum are to be applauded, it would be wrong to give workers the flexibility to retire when they want to. Scrap compulsory retirement ages and the circumstances in which long-serving employees end their working days would certainly change. They would leave with the sack instead of presentation and goodwill. The end point of the employer-employee relationship must be defined ...

Here is a weak answer to the question.

David McQueen says they would retire with dignity but Lisa Newman says they will be sacked.

Why is this answer weak?

This answer is weak because there is no reference to the question and no quotations from the sources to show the views.

Here is a better answer.

In Source A, David McQueen states that people 'could now retire with dignity' if compulsory retirement ages were abolished. Whereas, in Source B, Lisa Newman has the completely opposite view that the end of compulsory retirement ages would mean an undignified end and people 'would leave with the sack instead of a presentation and goodwill.'

Why is this answer better?

This answer is better because the sources are referenced, the views are quoted and the contrast between them is made clear.

> Remember, when answering evaluating questions ….
>
> – Use only the sources you are directed to in the question.
> – Use all the sources you are directed to in the question.
> – Do not add any extra knowledge and understanding.
> – Write a short answer giving main points only.
> – Make sure you name and quote evidence from the sources.
> – Make sure you give both sides in a 'to what extent' question.
> – Spend no more than 20 minutes.

THE DECISION MAKING TASK

The Decision Making Task should be written in a report style, and not as a 'for' and 'against' essay.

Principal Assessor's Report

The second part of Paper 2 is your Decision Making Task.

How much time should I spend on my Decision Making Task?

You should spend 40 minutes on your Decision Making Task. Part of this time should be for your planning. This is vital: do not miss it out!

What do I have to do?

You have to take on a role and write a report recommending a course of action, and provide information from the sources and your background knowledge to support it. You also have to identify and comment on any opposition to your recommendation.

What kind of role might I have to play?

You might be a researcher, an adviser, a civil servant, a consultant, a chairperson of a committee, a planner or an expert in social policy.

How do I know what my task is?

On the reverse side of your evaluating questions will be information like this about your task and the role you have to play.

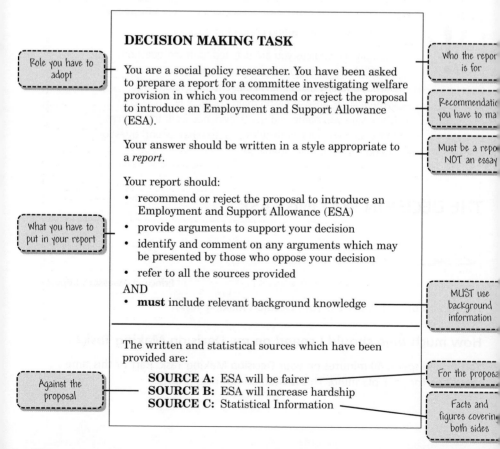

Role you have to adopt

DECISION MAKING TASK

You are a social policy researcher. You have been asked to prepare a report for a committee investigating welfare provision in which you recommend or reject the proposal to introduce an Employment and Support Allowance (ESA).

Who the report is for

Recommendation you have to make

Your answer should be written in a style appropriate to a *report*.

Must be a report NOT an essay

Your report should:

What you have to put in your report

*   recommend or reject the proposal to introduce an Employment and Support Allowance (ESA)
*   provide arguments to support your decision
*   identify and comment on any arguments which may be presented by those who oppose your decision
*   refer to all the sources provided

AND

*   **must** include relevant background knowledge

MUST use background information

The written and statistical sources which have been provided are:

Against the proposal

SOURCE A: ESA will be fairer

SOURCE B: ESA will increase hardship

SOURCE C: Statistical Information

For the proposal

Facts and figures covering both sides

Read the instructions carefully. Not all Decision Making Tasks are the same. Make sure you understand your task and know what you are expected to include in your report.

Make sure you understand your role. Do you have to be impartial? For example, are you a neutral civil servant adviser or researcher giving a balanced opinion of the pros and cons? Or do you have to adopt a point of view? For example, are you a director of a pressure group preparing a report from the point of view of the group or a parliamentary private secretary preparing a report from the point of view of the government?

Whatever your role, you must not be one-sided. You must **always** include other options and points of view in your report.

How do I show that I understand my role?

Refer to your role where appropriate in your report. For example, refer to your role at the start of your report and in your introduction.

Here is an example of how to layout an introduction.

	THE INTRODUCTION OF AN EMPLOYMENT AND SUPPORT ALLOWANCE (ESA)
	To:　Chairperson of the Committee Investigating Welfare Provision
	From:　Joe Bloggs, Social Policy Researcher, Scottish Institute of Social Policy
	Introduction
	In my capacity as a social policy researcher, I have been asked to make a recommendation on the proposal to introduce and Employment and Support Allowance (ESA) ...

Refer to your role in your conclusion and sign your report with your name and role.

Here is an example of how to layout a conclusion.

	Conclusion
	As a social policy researcher, it is my conclusion that ...
	Joe Bloggs,
	Researcher
	Scottish Institute of Social Policy
	20/05/20—

PLANNING THE REPORT

The sources always contain a number of succinct references to relevant background knowledge issues, which candidates may expand on.

Principal Assessor's Report

To plan your report you have to know which sources are balanced or biased, for or against the proposal, and completely factual or containing opinions.

Biased sources are usually statements by spokespersons or political parties, newspaper reports or letters. Balanced sources are usually the statistical sources and some research reports.

Reread the sources carefully and look for:

- arguments for and against the proposal
- headings to divide up information
- links between the sources
- clues to background information

Make notes of what you intend to put into your report. There are several ways you can make notes. You may decide to underline or highlight and make notes in the margin like this:

EXAM EXAMPLE

SOURCE A: ESA WILL BE FAIRER

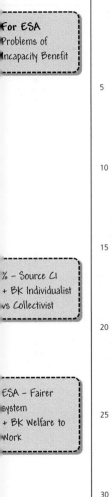

Incapacity Benefit is meant to provide an income for people who are unable to work because of medical reasons. It is the single most costly benefit that applies to people of working age. The
5 number of people claiming Incapacity Benefit has grown to 2.7 million. Most, but not all of these claimants, are genuinely disabled or suffering from a health condition that prevents them from working. In Scotland, over 300,000 people receive
10 Incapacity Benefit. In Glasgow, one in five of those of working age claim this benefit. Incapacity Benefit increases after six months and again after a year. It is paid for life and may be accompanied by other benefits. Incapacity Benefit discourages
15 people from seeking work. No wonder long-term sickness and disability is the most common reason given by both men and women for not working. It is not just older workers who qualify for Incapacity Benefit — each month over a thousand
20 teenagers claim it. We are encouraging welfare dependency at the expense of individual responsibility. Incapacity Benefit needs reform.

Our proposed Employment and Support Allowance (ESA) will be fairer to new claimants
25 and give the taxpayer better value for their money. It will pay more than Incapacity Benefit but new applicants will face rigorous medical tests to prove that they are entitled to it. Those judged capable of work will have to attend "work-focused
30 interviews" and take part in "work-related activities". At these interviews employment advisers will be available to help place people in appropriate employment. Claimants who refuse to attend for interview will have their payments cut.

Continued on next page

Against
Most claimants
genuine

Wrong about
women – Source
C1

101

35   Those who take up employment will qualify for
     extra benefits. The practice of increasing benefits
     over time will be scrapped.

     The UK already spends a greater percentage of its
     Gross Domestic Product (GDP) on schemes for
40   disabled workers than any other country in the
     European Union. We are determined to continue
     to move people from welfare into work. Our
     proposed reform should lead to a million fewer
     Incapacity Benefit claimants by 2016. The social
45   and economic benefits of work to the individual
     are obvious. New technology ensures that work is
     now less physically demanding. Savings made
     from the reform of Incapacity Benefit will, of
     course, be welcome. However, our main aim is to
50   return to the fundamental principles of the
     welfare state. It is surely far better to help people
     into the workplace than to condemn them to a life
     on benefits!

     Russell Barclay, Department for Work and
     Pensions (DWP) Spokesperson

Benefits of ESA
Savings – Source
C3(a) + BK
Benefits of Work
Principles of
Welfare State

Wrong about GDP
– Source C2 (a)

Or you may decide to use bullet points like this.

EXAM EXAMPLE

SOURCE B: ESA WILL INCREASE HARDSHIP

In the UK today, more people than ever are in
need of support from public funds. There are 7
million people of working age with either a
mental or physical disability.   Charities raise
5   millions of pounds to plug the income and health
gaps in the welfare state. They already spend
more on the disabled than on any other group*. Yet
surely it is the responsibility of the state — not
charities — to support people in need. There may
10   well be 2.7 million who claim Incapacity Benefit
but the number actually receiving Incapacity
Benefit fell from 1.9 million in 1995 to 1.7 million
in 2004, as so many claimants are turned down.
This shows how tough the rules are already.
15   Politicians should not complain about the cost of
the welfare state, and certainly never about
Incapacity Benefit. During the 1980s, it was
government policy to encourage people to claim
Incapacity Benefit in order to hide the true level of
20   unemployment. Now, the Government will
increase hardship by discouraging people from
claiming a benefit to which they should be
entitled. Disability experts forecast big problems
in deciding who is fit enough to work. Mistakes
25   will be made. Many claimants will be unable to
cope with the stress of attending interviews.
Others will be pressed into taking and keeping
jobs for which they are neither physically nor
mentally fit. It is disgraceful that those with
30   disabilities, and other groups vulnerable to
poverty, such as lone-parents, are being forced into
employment situations that they are unable to

Continued on next page

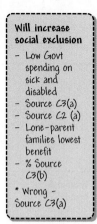

**Will increase
social exclusion**

- Low Govt
  spending on
  sick and
  disabled
- Source C3(a)
- Source C2 (a)
- Lone-parent
  families lowest
  benefit
- % Source
  C3(b)

* Wrong -
  Source C3(a)

cope with. "Welfare to Work" policies are clearly
more about saving money than meeting needs. We
35 live in an unequal society where there are
obstacles to employment for many disabled
people. Around a million people who want to work
cannot find jobs, as employers are reluctant to
take on staff with disabilities or other health
40 problems. UK Government spending on the sick
and disabled is already <u>lower than for any other
group</u>* and a lower percentage of one-parent
families receive Incapacity/Disability Benefit than
any other benefit.   Effective laws to prevent
45 discrimination against the disabled would be far
more useful than making the rules for Incapacity
Benefit even tougher. We fully support any
proposals that help disabled people to get jobs but
we totally oppose this proposed reform of
50 Incapacity Benefit. An Employment and Support
Allowance (ESA) will only lead to more social
exclusion and undermine the collectivist
principles of the welfare state.

Irene Graham, Disability Support Group (DSG)
Spokesperson

**Effective anti-
discrimination
laws would be
better**

- Obstacles to
  employment
- Im who want to
  work can't

BK - Social
Exclusion
Principles of
Welfare State

EXAM EXAMPLE

Statistics are often overlooked by candidates as giving them opportunities for development.

Higher Modern Studies DME Exemplars

Source C1: Reasons given by people of working age for not working

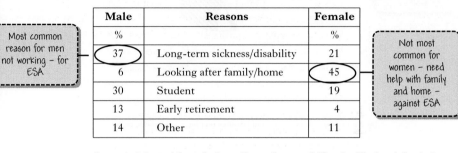

Male	Reasons	Female
%		%
37	Long-term sickness/disability	21
6	Looking after family/home	45
30	Student	19
13	Early retirement	4
14	Other	11

Most common reason for men not working – for ESA

Not most common for women – need help with family and home – against ESA

Source: Adapted from Labour Force Survey, Office for National Statistics

Source C2:

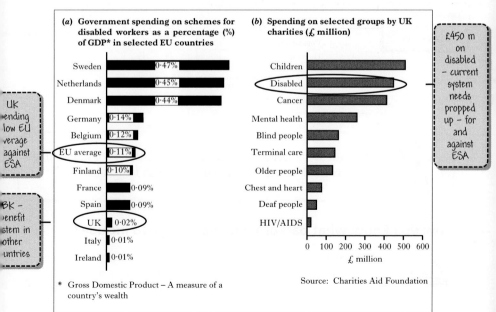

(a) Government spending on schemes for disabled workers as a percentage (%) of GDP* in selected EU countries

Sweden	0·47%
Netherlands	0·45%
Denmark	0·44%
Germany	0·14%
Belgium	0·12%
EU average	0·11%
Finland	0·10%
France	0·09%
Spain	0·09%
UK	0·02%
Italy	0·01%
Ireland	0·01%

(b) Spending on selected groups by UK charities (£ million)

Children
Disabled
Cancer
Mental health
Blind people
Terminal care
Older people
Chest and heart
Deaf people
HIV/AIDS

0 100 200 300 400 500 600
£ million

* Gross Domestic Product – A measure of a country's wealth

Source: Charities Aid Foundation

UK spending low EU average against ESA

UK – benefit system in other countries

£450 m on disabled – current system needs propped up – for and against ESA

Source C3:

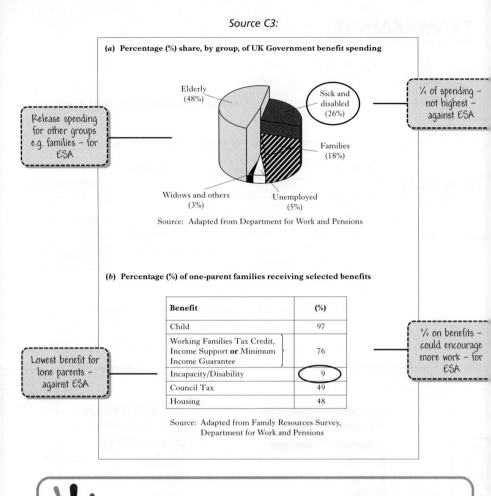

(a) Percentage (%) share, by group, of UK Government benefit spending

Release spending for other groups e.g. families – for ESA

Elderly (48%)

Sick and disabled (26%)

¼ of spending – not highest – against ESA

Families (18%)

Widows and others (3%)

Unemployed (5%)

Source: Adapted from Department for Work and Pensions

(b) Percentage (%) of one-parent families receiving selected benefits

Lowest benefit for lone parents – against ESA

Benefit	(%)
Child	97
Working Families Tax Credit, Income Support **or** Minimum Income Guarantee	76
Incapacity/Disability	9
Council Tax	49
Housing	48

¾ on benefits – could encourage more work – for ESA

Source: Adapted from Family Resources Survey, Department for Work and Pensions

> Look back at the section on data handling in Chapter 1 if you need to remind yourself how to quickly find information from data.

How do I know what background knowledge to include?

Candidates did not always appropriately develop source hints at use of background knowledge … identify and use source references for the purpose of integrating 'background knowledge' into the report.

Principal Assessor's Report

The written sources contain 'triggers' – key words or phrases that should alert you to what background knowledge to include.

Here are examples of 'triggers'.

> We are <u>encouraging welfare dependency at the expense of individual responsibility</u>.   *Source A*

> Yet surely it is the <u>responsibility of the state</u> – not charities – <u>to support people in need</u>.   *Source B*

These statements appear in the first paragraph of each of the sources and are a clue that the debate about whether the individual or the state should be responsible for welfare provision will be a source of background knowledge for the report.

Here is an example of how to use a 'trigger'.

> Savings made from the reform of Incapacity Benefit will, of course, be welcome. However, our main aim is to <u>return to the fundamental principles of the welfare state</u>.   *Source A*

The phrase 'fundamental principles of the welfare state' is a clue for you to bring in background knowledge about the original values of the welfare state – the state taking responsibility for tackling the 'five giants' with a collectivist, universal, non-means tested approach. You can use this information in your report to assess the claim made in Source A. You can also link it to the opposite claim in Source B that:

> An Employment and Support Allowance (ESA) will only lead to more social exclusion and <u>undermine the collectivist principles of the welfare state</u>.
>   *Source B*

Here is another example of how to use a 'trigger'.

> It is surely far <u>better to help people into the workplace than to condemn them to a life on benefits</u>!   *Source A*

This is a clue for you to use background knowledge about Welfare to Work policies like the New Deal, especially the New Deal for the Disabled, and use it to judge this statement. You can also link it with the claim in Source B that:

> 'Welfare to Work' policies are clearly more about saving money than meeting needs.
>
> *Source B*

Both statements then become a 'trigger' for background knowledge about policy differences within the Labour Party over the reform of Incapacity Benefit.

Practise looking for 'triggers' in the sources and try to include background knowledge under each of the headings in your report.

How can I organise my information?

Reports that have no background knowledge will not pass … integrate 'background knowledge' into the report: avoid a stand-alone 'background knowledge' section.

Principal Assessor's Report

You must make sure you synthesise (bring together) information from the written sources, statistical sources, background knowledge and then organise it under headings in your report.

You may want to use a table to make sure you include all the information you can.

Recommendation = Introduce ESA

Source	Support	Heading
A	Single most costly benefit – 2.7 million claim – over 300,000 in Scotland – 1 in 5 in Glasgow ...	Problems of Incapacity Benefit
C1	37% of men give long term sickness or disability as reason for not working	
BK	National Audit Office – on Incapacity Benefit more than 2 years are more likely to die or retire than get another job ...	
	Problems	
A	Most claimants genuine ...	Problems of ending Incapacity Benefit
BK	Problems with Back to Work schemes	
	Solutions	
A	Some claimants not genuine – work is better than benefits	Problems of ending Incapacity Benefit
BK	Welfare to Work schemes (New Deal) already in existence	

This is just the start of the planning table for the exam example. You can find the full version in the appendix at the end of the book.

How do I know what sub-headings to use?

Usually each paragraph of the written source will give you a topic for a heading. For example, in Source A the paragraphs are about:

> Paragraph 1 – Problems of Incapacity Benefit
>
> Paragraph 2 – The ESA is a Fairer System
>
> Paragraph 3 – Benefits of ESA

You could use these as sub-headings for one of the sections of your report.

How do I layout my report?

You will notice that you can get a layout for your report from the information you are given in the exam paper.

You could structure your report like this.

Title

To:

From:

1.0 Introduction
State what you have been asked to do …
Briefly explain the issue …
Give your recommendation …

2.0 Reasons for your recommendation
2.1
2.2 Give (develop) arguments in support of your recommendation …
2.3

3.0 Problems
3.1
3.2 Give (identify) arguments against your recommendation …
3.3

4.0 Solutions
4.1
4.2 Rebut (give answers to) and comment on opposing arguments …
4.3

5.0 Conclusion
Restate your recommendation …
Briefly summarise why the advantages of your recommendation outweigh the problems…

Signature

Role

Side notes (left):

Make sure you state your role and recommendation

Use a separate heading for each reason, problem or solution

Flag your sources by quoting the source number in the margin

Side notes (right):

Use the sources and background knowledge to explain your reasons, problems and solutions

For each written source try to find figures from statistical source to back up your point of view...

Solutions should directly link to, and answer, the problems

You must keep track of your use of sources and background knowledge. It is a good idea to tick off each source as you use it.

Source	A	✔
	B	✔
	C1	✔
	C2	✔
	C3	✔
Background Knowledge	(BK)	✔

WRITING THE REPORT

Use a report style in response to the task, and, where possible, feature 'source' and 'background knowledge' annotations in the margin.

Principal Assessor's Report

How do I write my introduction?

Give your recommendation and make it clear that you understand your role and task. Use the instructions in Question 4 – Decision Making Task to help you with this.

EXAM EXAMPLE

This introduction is weak.

> Introduction
>
> I am a social policy researcher. I have been asked to prepare a
> report for a committee investigating welfare provision in which I
> will recommend or reject the proposal to introduce an
> Employment and Support Allowance (ESA).

Why is this introduction weak?

The introduction is weak because it personalises and does not give a recommendation. It is copied almost word for word from the question and gives little indication that the role or task is understood.

> **! ! !**
> **! •**
>
> In your report avoid overuse of the word 'I'.

Here is a better introduction.

	1.0	Introduction
		As a social policy researcher, I have been asked to prepare a
		report on the proposal to introduce an Employment Support
		Allowance (ESA) for the Committee Investigating Welfare. The ESA
		proposal is controversial because it involves ending the current
		Incapacity Benefit for the sick and disabled. The plan is to
		replace it with a more rigorous Employment and Support
		Allowance which aims to get as many people as possible from
		benefit to work. There are strong views on both sides and the
		Department for Work and Pensions and the Disability Support
		Group statements contain some bias and exaggeration. However,
		there is enough impartial evidence to make a recommendation.
		After examining the sources and considering other relevant
		information, it is my recommendation that an Employment and
		Support Allowance (ESA) be introduced.

Why is this introduction better?

The introduction is better because it shows a clear understanding of the role and task. It briefly explains the issue and it is aware that is a controversial one. It also discerns bias in some of the sources and takes this into account. It gives a clear recommendation.

How do I provide arguments in support of my recommendation?

Excellent answers combine style with synthesised use of sources, very well integrated background information and well written conclusions.

Principal Assessor's Report

You are writing a report, not an essay. You **must** use a report style. Organise your information under headings with bullet points or numbering. Often each paragraph in the written sources will have a heading trigger. Each main point should have **synthesis** – information from more than one source, or a source and background knowledge. **Acknowledge** your sources by identifying and labelling them. **Verify** your statements with statistics from the sources or your background knowledge and point out any bias or exaggeration. Providing arguments is more than just copying information from the sources. You must **evaluate** by explaining why it is useful and showing how it advances the argument. You should also come to a conclusion about what the information shows.

SAVE

Synthesise	–	organise information under headings; connect sources and background knowledge
Acknowledge	–	label sources; identify background knowledge
Verify	–	prove statements with statistics; point out bias or exaggeration
Evaluate	–	explain usefulness of information; show how it advances argument; come to a conclusion

---

Look back to Chapter 1 for information on how to synthesise if you need a reminder of how to do this.

EXAM EXAMPLE

This is a weak argument in support.

> Incapacity Benefit is meant to provide an income for people who are unable to work because of medical reasons. It is the single most costly benefit that applies to people of working age. In Scotland, over 300,000 people receive Incapacity Benefit. In Glasgow, one in five of those of working age claim this benefit. Long-term sickness and disability is the most common reason given by both men and women for not working. Incapacity Benefit needs reform.

Why is this argument weak?

This argument is weak because it has no heading and does not acknowledge the source. Information is simply copied from the source with no attempt to organise it, explain its usefulness or show how it advances the argument in support of the recommendation. There is no synthesis – only one source is used and there is no linking information from other sources or relevant background knowledge. It contains incorrect information because the sources do not support the view that long-term sickness is the most common reason for women not working. It is not written in the style of a report.

Here is a better argument in support, but it still has some flaws.

> Incapacity Benefit needs to end because government spending on the sick and disabled accounts for 26% of government benefit spending (Source C3) and out of this Incapacity Benefit is the single most costly benefit (Source A). Over 2.7 million people claim it, with over 300,000 in Scotland and 1 in 5 in Glasgow alone (Source A). It discourages people from working because it

Continued on next page

	increases after six months, it is paid for life and entitles people
	to other benefits (Source A). In fact, it is the most common
	reason for men not working (Source A). 37% of men give long
	term sickness or disability as their reason for not working
	(Source C1) and at 21% the figure is pretty high for women too
	(Source C1).

Why is this argument in support better?

This argument is better because there is synthesis. Information from different sources is linked and statistical sources are used to verify written sources. This time the writer avoids exaggeration and skilfully uses the correct information from the sources to support the argument. There is an attempt to evaluate by showing the usefulness of the information.

What flaws does this argument have?

This paragraph could be part of an essay and this is not acceptable in Paper 2. Information must be organised under headings and presented in the style of a report. The paragraph does not clearly show how the information advances the argument. In fact, it is very difficult to tell what the recommendation is. The paragraph does not contain any background knowledge.

Here is a much better argument in support.

2.1	<u>Problems of Incapacity Benefit</u>
	One of the main reasons that an Employment and Support Allowance should be introduced is that the current Incapacity Benefit system has major problems, including:
	1. High level of cost
	According to the Department of Work and Pensions (DWP), the

Continued on next page

(Source C3) **A**	sick and disabled account for just over a quarter (26%) **V** of Government benefit spending and Incapacity Benefit is the "single most costly" benefit that applies to people of
(Source A)	working age. **S** As if this statistic was not worrying enough, a look at the high number of claimants shows that the cost of providing Incapacity Benefit is not likely to fall in the near future. **E**
	2. High numbers of claimants
	Figures from the Department of Work and Pensions (DWP) show that 2.7 million people in the UK claim Incapacity
(Source A) **A**	Benefit. In Scotland the figure is 300,000 and in Glasgow alone the DWP statistics show a staggering one in
(Source A)	five people of working age are claimants. This means that
(BK)	20% of the working population of Scotland's largest city claim they are unable to work for medical reasons. **E** The DWP contends that long term sickness and disability
(Source A)	is the "most common" reason for men not working. This is confirmed by the Office of National Statistics Labour Force
(Source C1)	Survey (LFS) which found that over one-third of males (37%) **V** gave this as their reason for not working. **S**
(Source C1)	This high number is not confined to men. The LFS found that just one-fifth (21%) of women also cited long term sickness and disability. Nor is this confined to the older generation. According to the DWP "thousands" of
(Source A)	teenagers are also claiming Incapacity Benefit. This means that in addition to meeting the high cost of Incapacity

Continued on next page

	Benefit, the country will face the prospect of a large
	percentage of its future working population not in
	employment due to medical reasons.
	3. Encourages welfare dependency
	According to the DWP, the way the Incapacity Benefit
(Source A) **A**	system operates actually "discourages people from seeking
	work". The benefit is paid for life and increases after six
	months and then again after a year. This guarantee of a
	rising income means people have very little incentive to look
	for work.
	According to the National Audit Office if people have been
	on Incapacity Benefit for more than two years they are
(BK)	more likely to "die or retire" than get another job. **S** Their
	statistics also show that this is not because claimants
	are "work-shy". They found that 90% of claimants wanted
(BK)	to return to work, but only 5% are actually supported by
	Back to Work schemes. **V** This shows the extent of the
	failure in the present system. **E**

Why is this argument in support much better?

The argument is much better because it uses a report style of headings and sub-headings. Information is synthesised **S** under each sub-heading by combining written sources, statistical sources and background knowledge. The source of information is clearly acknowledged **A** in the margin. Evidence is verified **V** by statistics from the sources or background knowledge. The information is evaluated **E** by converting it to give emphasis, explaining what it shows and coming to a conclusion about how it advances the argument.

Remember, you must evaluate your evidence by commenting on its usefulness, linking back to your recommendation and showing how it advances your argument. Look back at the section in Chapter 1 if you need to remind yourself of how to do this for statistical sources.

How do I identify and comment on opposing arguments

Some candidates have difficulty with the instruction 'identify and comment on any argument which may be presented by those who oppose your recommendation.'

Principal Assessor's Report

You do this in two stages:

1 Identify – state problems with, or opposing arguments to, your recommendation.

2 Comment – rebut by providing solutions and counter arguments.

EXAM EXAMPLE

Here is a very good paragraph identifying an opposing argument.

	3.1	Problems of ending Incapacity Benefit
		Opponents of ESA argue that scrapping Incapacity Benefit will do more harm than good because:
		1. It will make an already tough system even tougher. **E** 7 million people of working age in the UK have some kind of mental or physical disability, yet only about one-third
(Source B) **A**		(2.7 million) claim Incapacity Benefit and the number is actually falling. In 1995 1.9 million received Incapacity
(Source B)		Benefit, compared with only 1.7 million in 2004. **V**

Continued on next page

	According to the Disability Support Group (DSG), this
(Source B)	shows "how tough" the rules already are. Even the DWP
(Source A)	admits that most claimants are "genuinely disabled". $\boxed{S}$

	2. Charities will have to plug the gap in state help. $\boxed{E}$
	Charities Aid Foundation (CAF) statistics show charities
(Source C2(b))	already spend £450 million on disabled. The DWP's claim
	that the UK has the highest government spending on
(Source A) $\boxed{A}$	on disabled workers $\boxed{S}$ is disproved by the CAF figures
	which show it is actually the second lowest in the EU.
(Source C2(a))	UK spends only 0.02% of GDP - very far behind Sweden
(Source C2(a))	which spends 0.47% of its GDP. $\boxed{V}$

	3. DSG claims that in the past, the Government encouraged
	people to claim Incapacity Benefit as a means of lowering
(Source B) $\boxed{A}$	the unemployment figures. The DSG implies that, by
	emphasising capability rather than benefit entitlement, the
(BK)	ESA has a similar aim. $\boxed{E}$ According to the DSG, the
(Source B)	government will be "discouraging people from claiming" and
(BK)	this will "increase hardship" by forcing people 'back to
	work'. $\boxed{S}$

Why is this paragraph very good?

This paragraph is good because it has an excellent report style and clearly identifies the opposing arguments. It links back to the argument in support by using a similar heading and combines sources to refer to it in the paragraph. $\boxed{S}$ The sources and background knowledge are acknowledged. $\boxed{A}$ The impact of problems is substantiated by information from the statistical sources $\boxed{V}$ and there is a full and frank discussion of possible problems associated with the recommendation. $\boxed{E}$ This reflects the impartiality necessary for the role of a researcher.

How do I comment on opposing arguments?

Candidates should always comment on (rebut) arguments against the chosen option.

Principal Assessor's Report

What is rebuttal?

Rebuttal is counteracting or disproving the evidence against your recommendation. Basically, you are trying to cancel out any problems you have identified with your recommendation.

> To get a good grade for your report, you must include a rebuttal section.

EXAM EXAMPLE

Here is a very good paragraph commenting on an opposing argument.

	4.0	Solutions
		4.1 ESA will not make a tough system tougher. According to
(Source A)		the DWP not all claimants "are genuinely disabled" or even
		suffering from any real condition. Indeed, the DWP claims
		many of them could be working which is exactly what the
(Source A)		ESA's "work focused interviews" will enable them to do. In
		this respect the ESA will expand and develop the good
(BK)		work of the New Deal for the Disabled job brokers. This
		voluntary scheme matches the skills and abilities of
		disabled people to the needs of employers and over a
		quarter of a million (260,000) disabled people are
		registered. Over half (57%) achieve "sustainable" employment
(BK)		According to the DWP, one of the most positive aspects of

Continued on next page

(BK)	the scheme is that it encouraged people to move off incapacity benefits. If so many disabled people are doing this on a voluntary basis, it is unlikely that they find the system "tough".

Why is this paragraph very good?

This paragraph is good because it links directly to the problem. It provides an answer that combines information from the sources and background knowledge. It is an effective rebuttal because it persuasively argues the case and provides a credible solution to the problem raised earlier in the report.

> Not all the rebuttal evidence is in the sources. There will be clues, but this is where you really need to use your background knowledge to provide realistic solutions to the problems you have identified.

How do I write my conclusion?

Your conclusion should:

1. Restate your recommendation
2. Prioritise your arguments

A conclusion is not a summary. It is a justification of your decision. Try to end with a confident statement in support of your recommendation.

EXAM EXAMPLE

Here is a very good conclusion.

	5.0	Conclusion
		Therefore, it is my firm recommendation that an Employment and Support Allowance should be introduced. **1** The body of evidence is in favour of this. Of particular note, **2** is the culture of dependency the current Incapacity Benefit creates.

Continued on next page

Large numbers of people dependent on benefit, with little or

no incentive to find employment, is wasteful in both human

and financial terms. The introduction of an ESA, with a 'Back

to Work' ethic, will directly tackle this social problem.

Furthermore, the rigorous approach will result in a reduction

in dubious claimants. The resultant saving will release

money to help other disadvantaged groups move out of benefits

and into employment. The introduction of an ESA will

therefore help people to help themselves. 3

Signed: Joe Bloggs

Researcher

Scottish Institute of Social Policy

Date

Why is this conclusion very good?

This conclusion is good because it immediately restates the recommendation 1 and emphasises that the writer strongly holds this view. It states that the evidence gathered in the report supports the conclusion, and prioritises 2 the main arguments. It avoids simply summarising the report. Instead, it states clearly and persuasively why the recommendation is the right one. It ends with a strong statement confidently backing the line of argument taken in the report. 3

MARKING THE REPORT

What advice does the SQA give?

The SQA says:

> Candidates should produce a response to the Decision Making Exercise that demonstrates knowledge and understanding and evaluating. The discussion of the issue should be balanced and include appropriate points of view and conclusions. The report should be structured appropriately and give a reasoned and balanced recommendation supported by evidence from the sources and from background knowledge.

You can 'translate' this into what markers are looking for.

Markers like ...		Markers dislike ...	
Report style with subheadings	✔	Essay instead of a report	✗
Recommendation in introduction	✔	Recommendation not highlighted	✗
Developed arguments	✔	Sources just restated	✗
Statistics used for development	✔	Statistics simply copied	✗
Good synthesis with all sources used	✔	Sources not integrated	✗
Sources annotated in margin	✔	Sources not acknowledged	✗
Good balance for and against	✔	Poor opposing arguments	✗
Well-developed, featured rebuttal	✔	Little or no rebuttal	✗
Developed, integrated background knowledge	✔	Anecdotal or stand alone background knowledge	✗
Conclusion justifying recommendation	✔	Summary instead of conclusion	✗

Does the SQA give advice about what makes a Grade A report?

Yes. The SQA says that a Grade A report should:

- Demonstrate skills of evaluating by:
  - relevant, accurate and well-developed evaluation of complex sources
  - balanced and well-developed analysis that includes appropriate and well-argued conclusions, points of view and relevant background knowledge

Can I get a list of what to include in a report for a good pass?

Yes. The following report marking grid shows you what achieves good marks in a report. Markers read through your report to decide if it is a pass before reading it again to give it a mark. Make sure your report style, synthesis and background knowledge will impress the marker on first reading.

The report is worth 20 marks and the marks for each grade are:

C	10 or 11
B	12 or 13
A	14 and above

Use the grid to mark your own reports. It is a good idea if you are not doing well in an area of report writing to look back at that section of this chapter and see how you can move up the grid from pass, to good pass to very good pass.

REPORT MARKING GRID

Pass	Good Pass	Very Good Pass
Introduction		
States role	Shows understanding of role	Adopts a role
Understands the task	Clearly explains the task and issue	Insightfully explains task and issue
Makes a recommendation	Gives convincing recommendation	Makes persuasive recommendation
Main Body		
Appropriate arguments in support of recommendation	Detailed, developed arguments in support of recommendation	Comprehensive, persuasive arguments in support of recommendation
Enough opposing arguments	Detailed opposing arguments	Complex opposing arguments
Answers opposing arguments	Confident rebuttal of opposing arguments	Comprehensive rebuttal of opposing arguments
Use of enough relevant sources	Detailed use of relevant sources	Extensive use of range of relevant sources
Clear balanced explanation of usefulness of sources	Developed, balanced arguments from sources	Well-developed, balanced arguments from sources
Sources acknowledged and linked appropriately	Sources acknowledged and linked in detail	Extensive reference to, developed links between, sources
Enough appropriate background knowledge	Detailed, relevant background knowledge	Extensive, persuasively linked background knowledge
Conclusion		
Linked to task and role	Clear link to task and role	Convincing link to task and role
Satisfactory justification of recommendation	Confident, balanced justification of recommendation	Persuasive, balanced justification of recommendation
Report Style		
Report structure with headings	Developed paragraphs under suitable headings and subheadings	Fully developed paragraphs under convincing headings and sub-headings

Continued on next page

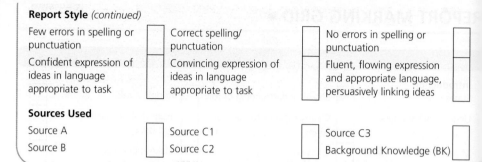

Report Style *(continued)*

| Few errors in spelling or punctuation | | Correct spelling/ punctuation | | No errors in spelling or punctuation | |
| Confident expression of ideas in language appropriate to task | | Convincing expression of ideas in language appropriate to task | | Fluent, flowing expression and appropriate language, persuasively linking ideas | |

Sources Used

| Source A | | Source C1 | | Source C3 | |
| Source B | | Source C2 | | Background Knowledge (BK) | |

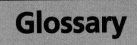
Glossary

Acknowledge – Point out the use of a source of information

Annotate – Highlight key information in the sources

Background knowledge (BK) – Knowledge included in your report that does not come from the sources provided; recall

Balanced opinion – Opinion that takes account of two sides of an argument

Bias – Only one side of an argument given

Comment – Express an opinion about a particular issue

Compare – Look for similarities

Conclusion – An opinion given after considering the facts

Contrast – Look for differences

Decision Making Exercise (DME) – Paper 2

Decision Making Task – Question 4 of Paper 2 where you adopt a role and write a report

Evaluate – Look at information to gauge its value, importance or usefulness

Evaluating questions – Questions in Paper 2 that require short responses using only the sources named in the question

Exaggeration – Over-emphasising the importance/lack of importance

Highlight – Draw attention to

Identify – Find something about a particular piece of information

Impartial – Unbiased; fair to both sides

Neutral – Unbiased; not supporting one side or the other

Persuasive – Presenting information in a way that convinces the reader

Point of view – Opinion

Quotation – Extract, in speech marks, using the exact words of the source

Read for information – Read with the purpose of finding specific information – searching out key words, phrases and statistics

Rebuttal – Solutions to the problems arising from your recommendation

Recommendation – Decision about what should be done

Role – Part you have to play when you write a report

Selective – Choosing to give only part of the information

Source – Text or data that gives information or evidence

Statistical information/evidence – Numerical information; data

Supporting a view – Providing evidence to back up a particular opinion

Synthesis – Combining ideas and information together from a number of different sources to strengthen a point

Verify – Prove something is true

Conclusion

With a solid grasp of the *Higher Modern Studies Grade Booster* skills and techniques you should be ready to realise your full potential. On the day of the examination, remember two things are really important – answering the questions as they are asked and managing your time. Unlock the questions, so you are very clear about what they are asking you to do. Divide your time sensibly so you do not find yourself rushing your fourth essay or your report.

By applying yourself to your Modern Studies course, you have developed skills to help you understand the world in which you live. You know how to gather information about important issues, how to analyse and evaluate that information, argue your viewpoint and influence decision making. But, most importantly, you know how to make up your own mind and come to your own conclusions. This critical thinking will not only help you in any further study of the social sciences, it will also help you take your place in society as an individual and a citizen.

Good luck!

ACKNOWLEDGEMENTS

We are grateful to our colleagues, especially Leeann Curran and Vicki McLaughlin, for generously sharing their experience. We also benefited from the light but steady guiding hand of Sarah, John and Fiona, our Leckie & Leckie editorial team. Finally, a big thank you to the Higher 'test pilots' of Braidhurst High School and Clydebank High School for their frank feedback!

"If I have seen further, it is by standing on the shoulders of giants."

Appendix

Recommendation = Introduce ESA		
Source	**Support**	**Heading**
A	Single most costly benefit – 2.7 million claim – over 300,000 in Scotland – 1 in 5 in Glasgow (lines 2 to 7)	1. Problems of Incapacity Benefit
	Most common reason for men not working - not just adults - thousands of teenagers claim - increases after 6 months and year – paid for life – get other benefits (lines 7 to 14)	
	Discourages people from working – encourages welfare dependency (line 14)	
BK	Increasing cost of welfare – finite resources, infinite demand	
A	Better value for money, pays more (lines 17 and 18)	2. ESA – Fairer System
	Rigorous medical tests, 'work focused interviews', 'work related activities', advisers (lines 18 to 21)	
	Payments cut if don't attend, extra benefits if employed, no increase over time (lines 23 to 25)	
BK	Welfare to work ethos - New Deal	
A	Savings from reform of Incapacity Benefit - reduce amount of GDP spent on disabled schemes (line 26)	3. Benefits of ESA
	1 million fewer claimants by 2016 (line 29)	
	Social/economic benefits to individual of work – return to fundamental principles of welfare state (line 31 to 35)	
BK	Benefits of work, principles of welfare state	
C1	Labour Force Survey, ONS - 37% men sickness/disability reason for not working	1. Problems of Incapacity Benefit

Continued on next page

C2(a)	Save cost of 0.02% of GDP spent on schemes for disabled workers	2. Benefits of ESA
C3(a)	26% - one-fifth of benefit spending is on sick and disabled – only 18% on families	2. Benefits of ESA
C3(b)	Only 76% - ¾ of lone parents on work related benefits	1. Problems of Incapacity Benefit
Problems		
A	Most claimants genuine (line 5)	1. Problems of ending Incapacity Benefit
B	7 million of working age with mental or physical disabilities - charities plug gaps (lines 2 and 3)	1. Problems of ending Incapacity Benefit
B	Responsibility of state to support people in need (line 5)	1. Problems of ending Incapacity Benefit
B	Tough rules - claimants turned down - 1.9m 1995 to 1.7m 2004 (lines 8 to 10)	1. Problems of ending Incapacity Benefit
BK	Original aims of welfare state	
B	Increase hardship - discourage claimants, mistakes, interview stress, forced into jobs (lines 23 to 25)	2. Disadvantages of ESA
	Increase social exclusion – low govt spending on sick and disabled – hits most vulnerable - unequal society (line 29 to 34)	
	Welfare to Work about saving money, hiding unemployment figures (line 12 to 14)	
BK	Extent/causes of poverty in UK	
B	Obstacles to employment for disabled – 1 million can't find work (line 30)	3. Anti-discrimination better
	Undermine collectivist principles of welfare state (line 40)	
BK	Political debate in Labour Party	
C1	Sick/disabled not most common for women – 45% – looking after family	2. Disadvantages of ESA
C2(a)	2nd bottom spending on disabled - well below EU average of 0.11% - 0.45% below highest Sweden	1. Problems of ending Incapacity Benefit
C2(b)	Over £400 million spent by charities on disabled	1. Problems of ending Incapacity Benefit

Continued on next page

C3(a)	Spending on disabled not biggest as claimed	1. Problems of ending Incapacity Benefit
C3(b)	Least common benefit for lone parents – 9%	2. Disadvantages of ESA
	Solutions	
A	Some claimants not genuine (line 4) – work better than benefits (line 35)	1. Problems of ending Incapacity Benefit
C3(a)	ESA would release disabled spending to spend on other groups like families	1. Problems of ending Incapacity Benefit
A	Advisers (line 22), new technology (line 33) – can cope with jobs	2. Disadvantages of ESA
BK	New Deal for the Disabled, 1980's dated – claimant count	2. Disadvantages of ESA
BK	Anti-discrimination laws, Welfare to Work	3. Anti-discrimination better

Line numbers refer to the Higher 2007 Paper